General editor: Graham Handley MA PhD

Brodie's Notes on Robert C. O'Brien's

Z for Zachariah

John Jenkins

MACMILLAN

First published 1988 by Pan Books Ltd

Reprinted 1992 by
THE MACMILLAN PRESS LTD
Houndmills, Basingstoke, Hampshire RG21 2XS
and London
Companies and representatives
throughout the world

ISBN 0-333-58161-X

Printed in Great Britain by
Clays Ltd, St Ives plc, Bungay, Suffolk

Contents

Page references are to the Heinemann Educational edition of *Z for Zachariah* but as references are also given to particular chapters, the Notes may be used with any edition of the book.

Preface by the general editor

The intention throughout this study aid is to stimulate and guide, to encourage your involvement in the book, and to develop informed responses and a sure understanding of the main details.

Brodie's Notes provide a clear outline of the play or novel's plot, followed by act, scene, or chapter summaries and/or commentaries. These are designed to emphasize the most important literary and factual details. Poems, stories or non-fiction texts combine brief summary with critical commentary on individual aspects or common features of the genre being examined. Textual notes define what is difficult or obscure and emphasize literary qualities. Revision questions are set at appropriate points to test your ability to appreciate the prescribed book and to write accurately and relevantly about it.

In addition, each of these Notes includes a critical appreciation of the author's art. This covers such major elements as characterization, style, structure, setting and themes. Poems are examined technically – rhyme, rhythm, for instance. In fact, any important aspect of the prescribed work will be evaluated. The aim is to send you back to the text you are studying.

Each study aid concludes with a series of general questions which require a detailed knowledge of the book: some of these questions may invite comparison with other books, some will be suitable for coursework exercises, and some could be adapted to work you are doing on another book or books. Each study aid has been adapted to meet the needs of the current examination requirements. They provide a basic, individual and imaginative response to the work being studied, and it is hoped that they will stimulate you to acquire disciplined reading habits and critical fluency.

Graham Handley 1991

The author and his work

Robert O'Brien is the pseudonym of Robert C. Conly who died in 1973, shortly after *Z for Zachariah* was published in America. He spent most of his working life on the staff of the *National Geographic Magazine*, a prestigious American publication known throughout the world. His work on this magazine, dealing with articles on a wide range of topics from ecology to oceanography, may be part of the reason for the underlying scientific thread in all of his books. As a writer, he produced four novels – *Z for Zachariah, Mrs Frisby and the Rats of Nihm, The Silver Crown* and *Report from Group 17*. Each of them may be termed 'science fiction', although he uses this genre to present stories which lead us to question the role of science in the modern world. His reputation rests principally on *Z for Zachariah* and *Mrs Frisby and the Rats of Nimh* (which won the Newbery Medal in 1972 and was later filmed as *The Secret of NIHM*). Both novels show O'Brien's rare ability to create compelling fictional worlds, not identical to our own, but similar enough to be disturbing. They are exciting adventure stories, but the reason for their enduring popularity lies in the fact that they can be read on deeper levels, as fairy stories or as allegories.

In 1986, his daughter Jane Leslie Conly wrote a sequel to *Mrs Frisby* entitled *Racso and the Rats of Nimh*. It received a mixed critical reception, one writer calling it 'a feeble copy of the original'. However, the thematic preoccupations are largely the same as those of the book which inspired it, and it is worth reading because of this.

Literary terms used in these notes

Archetype An archetype is a word used for an original or first model.

Flashback A flashback is a scene inserted into a television story, film or novel showing events which happened at an earlier time.

Genre A type or category. Some literary genres are: tragedy, comedy, epic.

Symbol Symbols in literature can be very complex, but at its simplest a symbol is something (it might be an object or an action) which represents not only itself but something else as well. A non-literary example might help here. If two Christians from different parts of the world saw a crucifix, they would see not only an object – two pieces of wood or metal arranged in a certain way – but what the crucifix represented: the life and death of Christ and the importance of the Christian message. The cross is a good example of a public symbol, public because its meaning is quite clear to everyone. Literary symbols can sometimes be more difficult to pin down because they work only in the book or poem in which they appear, and the author does not make things easy for us by telling us that they are symbols. Apple blossom, for instance, does not have the same public symbolic significance as the cross. We do not automatically feel that it 'stands for' something else. However, if we read *Z for Zachariah* carefully, we cannot help noticing that the fragrant apple blossom is associated with Ann's thoughts of marriage to Mr Loomis. Once we have become aware of the association – which is implied but never stated – between the apple tree and Ann's hopes, any further mention of it will prompt us to think of Ann. That is, while always remaining an apple tree, it also becomes a symbol of the way Ann feels, and the developing disappointment of her hopes. In Chapter 12, after she has discovered that Mr Loomis is a murderer, we learn that the apple blossom has wilted, and later, when she is on the run, that the tree is bearing fruit. It is a crab-apple tree and so the fruit will be bitter. The careful reader makes the connection between the wilting blossoms, the bitter fruit and what they symbolize – Ann's disappointment and subsequent danger.

Z for Zachariah
Background and plot

For more than a year, sixteen-year-old Ann Burden has lived alone on the family farm in Burden Valley, believing herself to be the sole survivor of a nuclear holocaust. By a miracle, Burden Valley escaped the fearful consequences of the war, except for a stream which has been contaminated.

One morning, Ann sees smoke on a ridge outside the valley, and realizes that she is not alone in the world. Her ambiguous responses to this are skilfully captured by the author; she is frightened because of the possible danger, yet consoled by the prospect of company. Deciding that caution would be wise, Ann tries to make the farm look uninhabited and retires to a cave in the woods. On the fourth day she observes unseen a solitary man approaching the farm.

Days pass, and Ann continues to watch the stranger from her vantage point. She sees him discover that there are two streams in the valley, one contaminated and the other clean. A little later, he is violently sick as he succumbs to the first signs of radiation sickness. Ann finds herself in an acute moral dilemma: the stranger frightens her, simply because he is a stranger in an empty and desolate world, and yet she cannot leave him to die. She decides to nurse him, and the rest of the novel devotes itself to studying the increasingly tense relationship she and Mr Loomis have. It begins quite promisingly. He is dependent upon Ann, who proves to be a capable and attentive nurse. Mr Loomis's former career makes him knowledgeable about the consequences of nuclear conflict but, more immediately important, enables him to make practical suggestions which will make running the farm that much easier. Yet while Mr Loomis is willing to talk about his work, he is reticent about one aspect of his life. It concerns a character called Edward whose name he cries out in his sickness. When Ann asks who Edward is, Mr Loomis becomes guarded, and in this way Robert O'Brien creates tension in the novel.

Ann innocently considers the possibility of marriage to Mr Loomis when he has fully recovered. However, before he has any hope of getting better, he will get much worse, and it is during the peak of his illness that the danger she is in becomes apparent. Returning from the fields one day, Ann finds Mr Loomis with a rifle which he fires into the house. With commendable courage, she refuses to panic, realizes that he is delirious and calms him down. Later he tells her he believed it was Edward he was shooting at. We share Ann's puzzlement: why would he wish to kill his friend? As his sickness deepens, we discover the truth about the situation Mr Loomis and Edward were in when the war started. Edward wishes to use the only radiation-proof suit to go and see if his family are still alive. That will leave Mr Loomis alone in the laboratory, stranded with no possible means of escape. It is a problem of nightmare proportions. To prevent Edward leaving, Mr Loomis shoots him, and it is the memory of these events and the guilt he feels which find release in Mr Loomis's delirium.

After his recovery, the relationship between Ann and Mr Loomis deteriorates. Now that he knows he is not going to die, his attitude towards survival becomes obsessive. He is still too weak to work, but Ann notices uneasily that he watches her rather as a master watches a slave. The balance of their relationship has changed, it is more sinister and suspicious. Neither fully trusts the other, and Ann watches his return to strength with dismay rather than joy.

His desire to dominate her is made most horrifyingly plain when he attempts to rape her one night. She manages to struggle free and escape to her cave. The novel now presents a tense struggle for power, a deadly game of cat and mouse. Mr Loomis captures Ann's dog, Faro, with the intention of using him to track her down. Yet Ann, always sensible and rational, realizes that they cannot continue living in such a way: they both need the food the farm produces and he is not yet strong enough to work hard. Yet Ann's wish to work on a co-operative, if not a personally friendly, basis is not shared by Mr Loomis. Concerned only with his own survival, he makes several attempts to capture Ann, even shooting to maim her, so that he can use her as a slave.

As Ann's plight becomes more desperate and she is a virtual prisoner in her own valley, she realizes that she must do something to resolve the situation. Her solution tells us a great deal about her. At no time does she consider shooting Mr Loomis, although that seems to be the only certain way of saving herself. Rather, she decides to leave the valley. She gains possession of the radiation-proof suit, for which Mr Loomis has already killed once. She manages to trick him away from the farmhouse, then appears before him wearing the safe-suit. Their final confrontation begins threateningly but ends amicably. With great courage Ann explains her reasons for leaving. The reader senses that despite Mr Loomis's early threats, he is more frightened of being left alone than Ann is, and it is fear of this which has prompted his actions. She turns from him, half expecting him to shoot her. Instead, he calls to her advising her to travel west. Ann does so, setting out through an unknown and barren landscape on her quest for a new life among new people. She does so with optimism.

Since 1973, when the novel was written, new ideas on what might happen after a nuclear war (such as the nuclear winter) have made it less likely that an entire valley could escape devastation in the way Burden Valley does. Even when he wrote the book, Robert O'Brien would have doubtless been aware that to stand at the very edge of the deadness as Mr Loomis does in the final chapter would be a very risky action given the ease with which radioactive dust is carried by the wind. However, it is essential to realize that this in no way diminishes the power of the novel. We will look more closely at this in the section entitled *Z for Zachariah and its genre*, but it is worth noting here that it is merely a device to get the story underway.

The title and its significance

In Chapter 7, Ann remembers learning the alphabet at Sunday school from *The Bible Letter Book*. It began 'A is for Adam' and ended 'Z is for Zachariah'. Because Adam was the first man, she recalls that as a child she believed Zachariah must be the last man. The implication behind this is clear within the context of the novel: if Adam was the first man upon earth, Mr Loomis is Zachariah, the last. But there is more to it than that, for Ann's reference to *The Bible Letter Book* puts the title into a religious, or semi-religious, context which makes us then ponder how Ann herself features in Robert O'Brien's scheme. Presumably if Mr Loomis is at the other end of creation from Adam, the first of men, then Ann is at the other end of the same creation from Eve, the first of women. In other words, Robert O'Brien seems to be presenting us with two people who are like Adam and Eve in that, so far as they know, they are the only people in existence. This is not to say that O'Brien is doing anything so crude as to make Ann a modern Eve and Mr Loomis a modern Adam. The connection is much more oblique than that. He does, however, seem to be taking one of the central features of the Biblical story and presenting his own version of it, from the other end of the time-scale. The use of the Adam and Eve archetype helps him to enrich and deepen the scope of the novel.

It makes us aware of the extreme circumstances under which Ann and Mr Loomis live. But their position is not unique, there is one extraordinary parallel, one other occasion when, according to the Bible, the earth was peopled by only two beings – the Creation. This gives us a helpful point of reference for it makes it that bit easier for us to assimilate the idea which O'Brien is presenting. At the same time it shows how starkly different are the lives of the first man and woman in Eden and the last man and woman in the valley. Firstly, Adam and Eve had a benign God watching over them who formulated simple, clear rules of conduct and punished them when they transgressed. In the bleak post-holocaust world of *Z for Zachariah*, there are no certainties and no laws. Strength and cunning, cruelty and selfishness are now assets in the struggle for life. Ann can appeal to no one to help her against Mr Loomis's harsh treatment. She is terrifyingly isolated. Secondly, Adam and Eve were alone on earth because no other human beings had been created: Ann and Mr Loomis are alone because a grotesque war has seemingly depopulated the planet.

Without pushing the Biblical parallel too far, we also see that it is helpful in another way. In the Bible God says 'It is not good that the man should live alone; I will make an helpmeet (companion) for him' (Genesis 2.18). If we discount the role reversal in *Z for Zachariah*, we see that, even though Ann is afraid of the stranger, she finds it *'companionable'* in Chapter 3 to have someone else in the valley. Later she smiles to think that together they might keep the world from dying. There are times when it seems their companionship can be mutually beneficial and they can salvage some sort of worthwhile life together. Ann nurses Mr Loomis through a critical illness; without her he would have died. He has the technical expertise to utilize what resources are left, and make life in the valley less arduous than it has been since the war. On one occasion, in Chapter 7 as they watch the sunset, he rests his hand on her shoulder in what seems like a friendly gesture, and the reader is aware of the simple but deep pleasure that can be found in shared experience. Sadly, of course, it does not last. Companionship brings misery and danger rather than fulfilment. Adam and Eve at least had each other when they were expelled from Eden; Ann leaves the valley alone.

Critical commentaries, textual notes and revision questions

Chapter 1
May 20–22

As well as covering the events of three days, the opening chapter also provides necessary background detail to explain the particular circumstances of what is happening in those three days, and in the rest of the book. On May 18th, Ann Burden saw the smoke of a camp-fire rising from behind Claypole Ridge, about fifteen miles from where she lives. The effect of this upon her is captured graphically in the two short, arresting sentences which open the book and which immediately convey her fear and the sense of threat the stranger, or strangers, represents. The reason for this becomes clear when she describes the conditions under which she lives. A year ago, nuclear war broke out, devastating the world outside her valley but leaving herself and her family miraculously untouched. When the war ended, her father, brother and cousin left the farm and made an initial sortie, returning with the news that no one in the area outside the valley was alive. The simple, undramatic way in which this horror is described conveys their shock far more effectively than a more graphic, sensational account.

They decide to make another sortie. This time none of them returns. Ann slowly realizes that she is the only person left alive – possibly in the entire world. This alarming fact is described compellingly in her straightforward account of the radio stations going off the air one by one, leaving her utterly alone. The hysteria of one particular radio announcer impresses itself deeply upon Ann, making her cautious of greeting any stranger. Marooned in a green and fertile valley just as surely as if she were cast away on a desert island, Ann's book is her dairy of events, designed to help her remain sane in her solitude.

The tension which is apparent in her first entry continues. On the second day, the smoke is closer, but still behind the ridge, indicating that the stranger has not yet discovered the valley. On the third day it comes from the same place. Ann methodically deduces what the stranger is doing – systematically searching to the east and west. The knowledge that someone else is alive evokes powerfully conflicting responses in her: relief that she is not alone in the world, and fear that the stranger might be as insane as the radio announcer. Cautious as always, she decides to hide in a nearby cave and observe the stranger before committing herself to greeting him.

I am afraid . . . that I am wrong Note how there is tension and uncertainty from the first. The two short, assertive sentences are followed by one which emphasizes Ann's unsureness and stresses her fear – she *prays* that she is mistaken.

dogwood A tree with large white or pink blossoms and scarlet berries.

Maybe he was beginning to be sick Ann uses 'sick' here in the American sense of illness. However, nausea is an early symptom of radiation poisoning. Mr Loomis is actually physically sick later in the novel.

the Dean Town road . . . County road 793 A State highway, called a 'Route', is rather like one of our main roads; a County road is like a smaller 'B' road. The precision with which these details are given helps to create a sense of reality. All of the places mentioned so far, Claypole Ridge, Odgentown and Dean Town, are fictional.

and everything will be all right again Note the sombre irony behind this statement. Ann is alone and wishes for company, yet ironically realizes that in a world now devoid of civilized standards, strangers might be dangerous. Of the two grim alternatives it is better to live in perpetual loneliness than to risk living with a stranger.

I was pretty sure I was the only person left in the world This overwhelming notion gains power from being expressed so simply.

I thought it was the batteries on my radio that had run down This statement poignantly illustrates Ann's complete isolation. The world beyond the valley is one she dare not enter. She has no means of knowing what is happening there.

He kept repeating his latitude and longitude Sailors in distress give their position when hoping for rescue. That the radio announcer should do this highlights his plight, but also, because of their nautical association, the words help clarify the nature of Ann's position. She is marooned.

He said some other things, too, that I did not like to hear She does not even write them down in her diary. Her reticence reminds us that it is only by closing her mind to some of the darker possibilities of life that she can sustain the determination to go on.

It also lets me know some things Ann's deductions in this paragraph show her to be both observant and intelligent.

the Amish Named after Jacob Ammann, the Amish are a Protestant group which originated in Switzerland. They are farmers and believe in simple living. They use horses to plough fields, and have no electricity or telephones. They settled in great numbers in Pennsylvania, one of the eastern states of the USA which is presumably where *Z for Zachariah* is set.

I am hoping to be an English teacher Ann's use of the present tense here reverberates for it is an ambition which now seems impossible to fulfil.

panel truck A lorry.

I don't go out there Once again, the enormity of the statement is underlined by its simplicity. Ann intended to leave the valley to become a teacher in the world outside. Now there is no world outside the confines of her valley.

Chapter 2
May 23–24

Ann describes in a methodical, systematic way her preparations to make the farm appear uninhabited. This precise detail in her writing reflects her personality generally. Evidently, the church plays an important role in Ann's life, for she mentions it early in Chapter 1 and again at the beginning of Chapter 2.

While she waits, Ann writes of her intention to calculate the date, for she is no longer sure of it. The details in her writing emphasize her isolation and the practical way in which she deals with it.

From the position of the stranger's camp fire, Ann is sure that he (she is convinced it is a man) has seen the valley, but his slow progress towards the farmhouse puzzles her – and us. Further important background detail is given of the water supply in the valley, important because of what subsequently happens to the stranger. There are two streams – Burden Creek, which is contaminated, and one farther from the farmhouse, which rises from deep underground and is pure. Ann describes her relief at discovering the fresh water of the other stream. It is a point she does not need to stress, for its implication is clear enough, and it serves as a reminder to the reader of the perilous nature of her life.

After some thought, Ann decides to climb Burden Hill early next morning to observe the stranger's approach more closely. Having decided this she is struck by a thought which she regards as foolish. If it is an official rescue party, which she will have to greet, her everyday clothes – men's jeans and a man's work shirt – are scarcely very elegant. Such personal vanity not only adds sympathetically to Ann's character, but also shows how such deeply ingrained features of human behaviour survive even a nuclear holocaust.

On May 24 the stranger finally appears. The chapter concludes with another note of drama being sounded – Ann has to decide whether to show herself or not.

(some of the boards are off the side – can I fix them?) Ann's attitude to the church and what it represents is an important thread running throughout the book.

It isn't really important, I suppose While accurate knowledge of time is no longer necessary, Ann's desire to know when her birthday falls is an important – and understandable – aspect of the human need to impose order on the world.

Another lucky thing was that the war ended in the spring It is part of Ann's nature to be practical and realistic. She could do nothing to prevent the outbreak of war, nor to aid the casualties. Her own plight is unenviable and it is an indication of her strength of character that she attempts to be constructive and hopeful rather than negative and despairing.

a cord of wood An old-fashioned term for a stack of wood about 8 feet by 4 feet by 4 feet.

bucksaw A type of heavy saw.

I've already put oil on all the bolts . . . Ann's plans to move the stove into the house ready for the winter are yet another example of her foresight and hardy self-reliance.

I feel as if it is the beginning of the end Ann has no sooner adjusted to a life of complete isolation than she undergoes another traumatic upheaval. However, the ominous note sounded by this sentence is contradicted by the final sentence of the book.

In fact the wood . . . I know them all Ann's deep knowledge of and affection for the valley in which she lives and has grown up is an important theme in the book, especially when we remember that she finally leaves it.

I am a good shot Another important accomplishment. Ann's life as a farmer's daughter has given her invaluable skills for survival.

like the wet suits skin divers wear The image is an apt one, providing a chilling reminder that the world beyond the valley is now as alien an environment for a human being as water is.

Chapter 3
May 24–25

Ann decides not to show herself to the stranger, deciding that caution is more prudent. Instead, as the stranger descends into the valley in the afternoon, she follows him at a safe distance observing his behaviour carefully. Note how proprietorial Ann is, almost expressing resentment that the stranger is in her house.

The chapter is concerned principally with presenting the stranger and showing his reactions to the valley which Ann records in great detail. Her own desperate need for company almost overcomes her caution, but prudence triumphs and she remains hidden. Her description of the stranger's appearance is interesting mainly for an additional detail it gives us about Ann herself. Practical and level-headed though she has shown herself to be, we begin to glimpse another, more sensitive side to her nature.

Having searched the house and found nothing to indicate that it is occupied, the stranger sets up his tent and cooks a meal. His caution, evident in the way he double-checked for radiation earlier on, is again apparent when he chooses to sleep in the radiation-proof tent rather than in the farmhouse. Satisfied that there is no more to see Ann retires to the cave, feeling apprehensive and yet consoled that she is no longer alone in the valley.

On the next day, the stranger makes an error which proves nearly fatal for him. After a meal, he sets off to round up the cows he has heard lowing. His caution is apparent in that he is still wearing his radiation-proof suit and tests the water in the uncontaminated pond before drinking it. After taking these precautions he swims in Burden Creek, clearly thinking it comes from the same source as the pond. As he does not know the geography of the valley, it is a pardonable mistake. Furthermore, because nerve gas and bacteria were used in the war it is not certain that the creek has been contaminated by radioactivity, so his Geiger counter might have been useless anyway. Ann holds herself partly responsible for what has happened, for she feels that she could not warn him without giving herself away. Already, the arrival of the stranger has presented her with a moral complication.

Then he stopped, and instead ran back to the wagon Although he sees green leaves and living trees, the stranger does not trust the evidence of his senses, and checks with a Geiger counter. His extreme caution is a feature he shares with Ann.

I wanted to cry, and touch his face . . . stayed quiet The deep emotion which wells up in Ann here shows how desperately she craves for human contact. Yet we notice, too, how quickly prudence stifles this sudden eruption of feeling. Ann is someone who feels very deeply, yet is not at the mercy of her emotions. Consequently, she rises in our esteem.

then he did a surprising thing . . . Then he began to act in a strange way His behaviour, of course, is surprising and strange only to Ann who knows that there is no one but herself in the valley and that she means no harm. From the stranger's point of view, he is being no more prudent than she is in hiding from him.

carbine A short rifle used by the cavalry.

square magazine The case holding the cartridges which is attached to the rifle and feeds bullets into the firing chamber.

bolt-action and mine is a pump Two ways of loading a rifle. A bolt-action has a sliding part resembling a door bolt which is moved back and fore to open and close the chamber for the cartridge. A pump-action has a cylinder which 'pumps' the cartridge into the beech. Notice Ann's knowledge of guns.

shooting is not the accepted method of killing a tame chicken A clue that the stranger does not come from the countryside.

rotated it to fescue Planted it with grass seed.

though the songbirds are all gone Making the silence in which Ann lives all the more unnatural.

'other anti-personnel weapons' A euphemism for other deadly weapons.

Chapter 4
Still May 25–May 26

Much to Ann's surprise, Faro, her cousin David's dog, returns to the farm. Ann thought he had followed David, and died in the wilderness outside the valley, but concludes that he had lived in the woods awaiting David's return. His appearance marks an important development in the plot, for after eating food that the stranger puts down for him, he finds Ann's tracks and bounds towards the cave. Ann realizes with horror that if the stranger manages to tame Faro her discovery will be inevitable. Her fear of the stranger leads her to contrast her former friendliness at school with her present suspicion and, more touchingly, to reflect on her prayer that a man would enter the valley to give her company and – later – children. Now, haunted by the memory of the crazed radio announcer, she realizes how naive such dreams were. This passage gently evokes Ann's natural longing for company and children. It also shows her understanding of the gulf between the idyllic future of which she had sometimes dreamed, and the dangerous path she must tread where a careless move could make her life even more unenviable than it is at present. She is acutely aware that the stranger is stronger than she is and, if he wished, could subdue her entirely, leaving her with no chance of escape. The return of Faro, who – significantly – loves to hunt, makes her, and the reader, more aware of this sinister possibility.

On Sunday Ann abandons her usual practice of visiting the church in the morning in order to follow the stranger as he explores the valley. He discovers that there are two streams. Ann presumes that he realizes he swam in contaminated water yesterday. If this is so his reaction is an interesting one, for he shows no sign of panic but strides on to the end of the valley. The further details Ann gives of the shape of this part of the valley are important. The valley is completely enclosed, a little world within a world, seeming to have even its own weather. This might account for its having escaped the lethal effects of radioactive dust. As he walks up the valley toward the farmhouse, the stranger shows signs of succumbing to the first symptoms of radiation poisoning. Exhausted and nauseous, he stumbles into his tent, too feeble to feed either himself or Faro.

and he loved to hunt Notice how this apparently incidental detail is merely mentioned here, leaving its more unpleasant implications to be explored later in the book.

I did not dare act too friendly Ann has to bring the same iron self-will towards her desire to welcome Faro as she does towards her wish to greet the stranger. Ironically, what she yearns for most – company – is that which might bring the greatest danger to her.

it is a dream, I know Dreams are very important to Ann. See Chapters 5, 24 and 26 for other examples.

and I will be a slave for the rest of my life The statement gains its power from the fact that it is not *hyperbole* (exaggeration for the sake of effect), but the simple, literal truth.

he looks almost handsome Ann's comment suggests more than the fact that she finds him quite attractive. Alert for any indication of the type of man he is, Ann sees his presentable appearance as a point in his favour.

as Sunday is supposed to be Another example of her religious nature, and also her wish to impose some sense of traditional order upon the otherwise extraordinary circumstances of her life.

Psalms and Ecclesiastes Books in the Old Testament.

But it may be that in the morning he will be better Ann perhaps rather hopes than believes this. If he is ill, she will have to decide whether to help him and therefore show herself sooner than she wished.

Chapter 5
May 27–28

After some deliberation, Ann decides that she must help the man. This decision is prompted by a dream she had in which firstly it was her father, not the stranger, who was ill in the tent, and then that her entire family were safe in the house. The dream is important for it clarifies in Ann's mind something which her conscious mind has been unable to decide. Before the dream, Ann feels that the death of the stranger would not be a grievous blow to her; after it, she is not so complacent. This is so because a dream allows one seemingly to experience an emotion as it happens – it is as if one were actually there – and so the sensation of joy she feels is almost overwhelming. In other words, in her dream she seems actually to experience the prospect of company rather than merely to imagine it or think of what it would be like. This joy contrasts cruelly with waking reality. It makes her realize, perhaps as nothing else could, that her craving for company is greater than her fear of what the man might do to her.

The man's first words to Ann make little sense as he is delirious, although they become increasingly significant, and alarming, as the novel progresses. Ann feeds him and visits him regularly during the night, so great is her concern that he should live. The following morning Ann tests the water in Burden Creek with a Geiger counter. It is, in fact, radioactive, despite what Ann thought in Chapter 3, and the man has received a severe, possibly fatal, dose. He is knowledge-able about the effects of radiation and as he explains to Ann how radiation damages the body, she notices the detached, almost clinical way in which he speaks. Even though there is little she can do to mitigate the radiation sickness, she determines to take the utmost precautions to prevent further debilitation from disease. She realizes that she does not know his name, but then we still do not know hers.

Although he likes me, he seems to be adopting the man Another seemingly incidental comment, the full importance of which only becomes apparent later on.

It began with a dream Another example of the way in which a dream influences Ann's thoughts.

I felt so joyful Once more, the statement is deceptive in its simplicity. It carries a deep emotional undercurrent in expressing the profound sense of sadness which Ann feels for the loss of her family. Ann Burden might be coping very well, but the reader is left in no doubt that this is because of her sheer determination to do so. The pure delight she feels when she dreams that her family are alive shows how deeply she misses them.

I began worrying about his being sick . . . quite desperate This marks a significant development in Ann's relationship with the stranger, even though she has yet to meet him. Chapter 3 ended with her hoping he wouldn't die, no more than that. Now the possibility of his death is scarcely bearable.

I had already decided to move back to the house . . . just in case Another example of Ann's caution, as is her decision a little later not to mention the cave.

anaemic Having a blood deficiency.

roentgen Named after the German scientist, a pioneer in work on radiation. The X-rays used in hospital are radiation rays discovered by Roentgen.

Those won't help, not now . . . intravenous nutrients The primitive nature of health care and medicine now available is implied forcefully in these lines. Intravenous feeding is the transmission of liquid nutrients directly into the blood stream.

Revision questions on Chapters 1–5

1 What aspects of Ann's character are introduced in the first chapter?

2 Outline briefly the stages by which Ann is completely isolated from the world as the radio stations go off the air. How does this affect her?

3 Attempt a character study of the stranger from what Ann tells us in Chapter 3.

4 Read Chapters 3 and 4 and list those occasions when Ann seems to feel a certain resentment that the stranger is making use of what belongs to her.

5 Trace the way in which Ann's attitude towards the stranger changes and develops in the first five chapters.

Chapter 6
May 29

This chapter provides important background detail on the stranger who feels temporarily well enough to tell Ann what had happened to him during and since the war. Equally significant there is the suggestion that he has not told the full story, and this sense of mystery spurs the reader to continue reading. It also suggests that Ann's cheerfulness at the beginning of the chapter might have been rather premature.

They exchange names and Ann discovers that the stranger, Mr Loomis, had been a research chemist working with a famous scientist on a project to produce a radiation-proof material. Because of the highly secret nature of the work, their laboratory was situated deep underground in the mountains and had been equipped as a nuclear shelter as an additional precaution. This saved Mr Loomis' life although his professor had been less fortunate as he had been away from the laboratory when war broke out and had presumably died. After a three month wait in the laboratory, Mr Loomis took the radiation-proof suit and began to explore the outside world. He describes his visit to a nearby Air Force base where there had been a desperate struggle involving military personnel and civilians as they fought for a place in a nuclear shelter. His account dramatically underlines the utter chaos to which the radio announcer had alluded in Chapter 1. However, those who had places in nuclear shelters enjoyed only a short-term safety. Fallout shelters contained limited supplies of food and water in the belief that after a while radiation levels would fall and it would be safe to leave the shelters. This had not happened. The fate of those people in such shelters is not mentioned by Mr Loomis, but is easily imagined.

The chapter ends with a surprising incident which makes the reader question the truth of Mr Loomis's story. Ann's innocent enquiry about Edward obviously startles Mr Loomis and we learn that, whereas his story had led us to believe only he and the professor were working on the project, there had been in fact three of them.

a chemist A research chemist.
Ithaca . . . Cornell University Ithaca is a city in New York State.

Cornell, one of the most famous universities in America, was founded in 1865 by Ezra Cornell.

I felt happy and excited Notice the change in Ann's attitude toward the stranger. She no longer feels apprehensive.

as if I . . . might be playing a trick on him A glimpse of Mr Loomis's vulnerability. Ann feels more secure than Mr Loomis does at this point. He is not only ill, but is in a strange place relying on the help of a strange person.

I was still expecting the deadness to creep in from outside Another simple comment which carries horrific undertones. The reader is left to imagine what Ann must have felt like in those first months after the war, not only having to face living alone, but possibly dying alone too.

'You can lean on me,' I said An image which sums up completely the nature of the relationship at present.

graduate student Mr Loomis had already graduated from university and was studying for a higher degree.

organic chemistry That branch of chemistry which examines the structure of plants and animals.

Nobel Prize Named after the Swedish chemist Alfred Nobel (1833–96), the Nobel Prize is awarded annually for the best work done in the fields of chemistry, physics, medicine, literature and peace.

cosmic rays Radioactive waves from outer space.

That was what the government . . . been atom-bombed Another hint that Ann strongly dislikes violence. In Chapter 2 she has already mentioned her dislike of guns.

Washington The capital of the United States.

the Pentagon Situated in Arlington, Virginia, the Pentagon is the headquarters of the American defence establishment. It is so named because the building has five sides.

asphyxiation Suffocation.

Because all of the underground . . . that had not happened This passage illustrates the dangers of the misuse of science, which is one of the principal themes of the book.

He relaxed . . . mentioned his name Notice that whereas Mr Loomis has told Ann what happened to Professor Kylmer, he says nothing of Edward's fate. He relaxes only when he feels Ann knows nothing more than she has said.

I got him another glass . . . had fallen This blunt sentence draws our attention ominously back to his stunned response when Ann first mentions Edward's name.

Chapter 7
June 3

On June 3rd Ann writes up the events of the past four days, a sequence which closes at the end of Chapter 10. Ann works in the vegetable garden, while Mr Loomis leaves his bed to watch her. His scientific background promises to be of great utility, for he suggests that the petrol pumps at Klein's store could be used manually to enable them to drive the farm tractor. Ann feels ashamed at not having thought of so obvious a possibility herself, but the episode shows that although she is practically minded in terms of planning the running of the farm, she is not mechanically minded. There are important indications in the chapter that their relationship is developing promisingly. Mr Loomis smiles at the fact that Ann had not thought of trying to use the petrol at Klein's store, and as they watch the sun setting he puts his hand on Ann's shoulder. However, there are two incidents which mar the idyll and make the reader uneasy about their future together.

The first comes after dinner. Even though she is tired, Ann feels she should try to relieve Mr Loomis's boredom and so tentatively offers to play the piano. His delight at the prospect of hearing music again is genuine, as is his appreciation at the end of the performance. But a simple query of Ann's brings an angry response. Ann's excuse for him – that he is ill and therefore likely to lose his temper – might of course be true. Still, it is a blemish upon the evening and one that neither Ann nor the reader forgets.

The second instance occurs after they have gone to bed. Ann is uncharacteristically despondent. She is upset by Mr Loomis's anger, but equally by memories awakened by the hymns she played for him. They are memories of family outings to Sunday School – a festive occasion for Ann – and of learning her alphabet there from *The Bible Letter Book*. The final entry – 'Z is for Zachariah' – gives the novel its title and alludes, of course, to Mr Loomis. Ann decides to spend the night in the security of the cave, but intends returning in the morning so that Mr Loomis would be unaware that she had gone. As she passes Mr Loomis's bedroom, she hears him arguing with Edward. It is another disturbing reminder of something which troubles Mr Loomis greatly, and of which he has told Ann nothing. She decides that he is too ill to be left alone even for the night and returns to her bed.

he was still in the 'interim' period Mr Loomis is in the 'middle part' of his illness. The worst is yet to come.

I wanted some left over for preserving Another instance of Ann's foresight.

noticing, I suppose, how messy I looked There is nothing to suggest that Mr Loomis's comment is anything more than a casual, objective comment, but Ann's concern with her appearance is a notable, and understandable, feature of her early relationship with Mr Loomis. She does, after all, consider him to be 'almost handsome' (Chapter 4).

he rested his hand on my shoulder This seems to be a gesture of friendship, for he walks the rest of the way without help.

Still, for the first time . . . I was always quite tired at the end of the day
Entertaining Mr Loomis is another responsibility Ann takes on. He exploits both when the relationship deteriorates.

Für Elise A piece by Beethoven.

I can play hymns better than anything else This comment, and subsequent ones about her visits to Sunday School, reveal her deeply religious attitude and the traditional nature of her upbringing.

'You heard me,' he said. 'I said "ever".' These words leave us puzzled about the kind of life Mr Loomis has lived.

Chapter 8
June 3 (continued)

This chapter deals with the events of June 1st. Ann awakens with an idea of how to make a salad from wild plants, having been inspired by a dream about her mother. While she is gathering the ingredients in the fields nearby, the stillness of the morning and the fragrant perfume of crabapple blossom conspire to make her think of marriage to Mr Loomis in a year's time – when the blossom returns to the crabapple tree. The prospect excites Ann, and leads her to dream of a future occasion when she will gather greens with her own children, just as her mother did with her. However, the memory of her mother turns a pleasant dream of the future into a melancholy reminder of what she has lost. With typical lack of self-pity, Ann pushes the thought from her mind.

On returning to the house, Ann discovers that Mr Loomis is not there. She finds him near Burden Creek, where he had gone to check that Ann's calculation of its radiation level was correct. She notices that he displays the same calmness and lack of fear having confirmed that it was correct as he did when she first told him. Despite this disappointment, he has been thinking of ways to utilize his technical knowledge. One obvious idea is to use water power to generate enough electricity to run a freezer and a refrigerator.

After breakfast we are given a startling reminder that Mr Loomis is still very ill when a short walk tires him. This makes Ann regard her early morning dreams of marriage and a happy future as self-indulgent. The chapter closes on a note of seeming domestic contentment. Ann takes particular trouble over preparing the evening meal, and later Mr Loomis reads manuals on how to build a generator. The incident shows the softer, more 'romantic' side of Ann's character and implies a contrast with the world of science and technology in which Mr Loomis seems at home.

poke greens Wild plants which yield succulent leaves.

the branches and all the white blossoms . . . an almost magic look An important example of Ann's aesthetic sense (her liking for beautiful things). She is so overwhelmed by the beauty of the crabapple blossoms that she sits in the wet grass to gaze at them. A love of, and need for, beauty is an essential feature of Ann's character.

junior high school Rather similar to a British 'middle' school, American children leave their junior high school at about 14.

those of us who came on the bus . . . hillbillies Further evidence of the traditional and rather prim nature of Ann's upbringing. It has, though, prepared her admirably to look after herself.

There *should* be a ceremony . . . with flowers Ann's wish for a 'normal' wedding is all the more poignant given the circumstances under which it would take place. However, it is not the incidentals of a wedding ceremony which attract her; it is the religious and moral seriousness of making certain promises before God. The passage shows Ann's devout nature.

lumber Pieces of wood.

your refrigerator, your freezer Mr Loomis still considers himself an outsider in Ann's home.

masonite A mineral found in Rhode Island which is rather like slate.

slick Smooth.

Thanksgiving The last Thursday in November. In America, Thanksgiving Day is a celebration rather like our harvest festival, to thank God for a plentiful harvest of crops.

They just did not look as romantic Ann is clearly still thinking of marriage to Mr Loomis, despite her earlier belief that such thoughts were self-indulgent.

Chapter 9
June 3 (continued)

This chapter deals with the events of June 2nd. Building a generator would be a long-term project but Mr Loomis's technical experience promises to bring more immediate reward. He shows Ann how to pump petrol manually from Klein's store and she manages to start the tractor. Although she is surprised by Mr Loomis's undemonstrative attitude towards her achievements, nothing can diminish Ann's joy. This is partly because the tractor will enable her to plough grassland more easily. But perhaps even more important is that it will make her more self-sufficient. It is only now that she can fully acknowledge a thought which was previously too painful to bear: that Klein's store is not a limitless source of supplies; and growing enough food to live on will become increasingly more difficult. The episode shows how perilous were Ann's chances of survival. Now all such thoughts are forgotten. Instead of having the role assigned to her by the lines of the poem – the person whose lot it is to record the death of the planet – she can now, with Mr Loomis, help it live a little longer. The crows which follow the tractor increase Ann's happiness for they are possibly the only wild birds left in the world. In addition, they provide Ann with a pleasing sense of continuity, for they follow the tractor now just as they had done before the war.

Ann's perfect day is blighted, however, when Mr Loomis's temperature reaches one hundred and four degrees. The climax of his illness has come.

crank A starting-handle.
squash A gourd rather like a pumpkin.
thresher . . . mill A thresher would separate the grain from the husks; a mill would grind it. Notice, once again, in this paragraph the invaluable knowledge Ann has of the practicalities of farming.
hominy Shelled sweetcorn which has been boiled with milk or water.
I am very fond of poetry Ann's love of books and poetry, and the imaginative enrichment they offer, is an important part of her personality, and something which distinguishes her from Mr Loomis.
Oh earth, unhappy planet . . . your confessor be The name of the author of this sonnet is not known.

Chapter 10
June 3 (continued)

This chapter completes the sequence begun at Chapter 7, and brings us up to date. It provides a marked contrast with the previous chapter in that Ann's happiness is replaced by her concern for Mr Loomis and, as we shall see, there are other, threatening, developments. The crisis of his illness begins and Ann does not realize at first that it has come, but when she does she responds calmly. In fact, they appear to undergo a role reversal: Mr Loomis, hitherto so detached about his illness, now becomes frightened; Ann, who had seemed to dread the prospect of his illness more than he did, discovers that she is self-controlled. It is an aspect of her character which is developed further a little later in the chapter.

After a while, Mr Loomis seems to regain his self-control. He jokingly chides Ann for sounding like a nurse, and even suggests that she must regret his coming to the valley. Ann is too shy to tell him her thoughts of that morning concerning marriage. Instead she tells that she knew Burden Creek was poisoned and wishes she had warned him against bathing it it. Mr Loomis does not seem to hold her in any way responsible. This part of the chapter presents a quiet, rather touching period in their relationship before describing the disturbing events of the next day, June 3rd.

Ann takes scrupulous and loving care of her patient, and it is not until the afternoon that events become more sinister. As she reaches the driveway of the house, Ann sees Mr Loomis run to his cart, produce a rifle and fire three shots into the house. Ignoring her own safety, Ann runs towards him, shouting, but he then aims the rifle at her. Ann's calmness surprises her, but she is in fact exhibiting the same self-control here that she showed earlier in the chapter, and will show again later when she confronts Mr Loomis for the last time. The fact that Mr Loomis is hallucinating here, and actually means Ann herself no harm, lessens neither her bravery nor the danger she is in. She has no way of knowing beforehand that her calm, reasoning voice will have any effect on him.

The episode re-introduces another factor which has been in abeyance for a while: Mr Loomis and the mysterious Edward. It is Edward whom Mr Loomis thinks he sees in the house; it is Edward whom he shoots at. Even at the end of the chapter, when Mr Loomis appears to be much calmer, he asks Ann whether Edward has gone. Mr Loomis's wish to shoot someone who is his friend puzzles Ann; the truth emerges in the next chapter.

Ann Burden As Ann notices, he uses her full name here and a little later, as if using her first name would be too presumptuous and calling her Miss Burden too formal. Yet it draws our attention to the fact that they scarcely know each other. Notice, too, that at no time does Ann refer to him by his first name alone. Although we learn Ann's surname in the early stages of the novel this is the first time her Christian name is revealed. This is natural given that the novel is apparently a private record of events.

But I worried about it anyway, and I still do Given the circumstances no one could blame Ann for keeping quiet – Mr Loomis certainly does not. But she has a highly developed moral conscience, and finds it less easy to forgive herself.

steeped Soaked.

But I now face a problem . . . milk the cow again This paragraph illustrates the onerous nature of Ann's responsibilities. There is literally no one to whom she can turn for help.

after he had recovered Ann refuses to consider the alternative possibility.

His face looked incredibly distressed and twisted up Mr Loomis is racked by guilt at having murdered Edward. Notice that he is evasive when Ann questions him, and only mentions Edward's name later when he has no choice. It is a secret too enormous to bear, yet too terrible to confide.

Revision Questions on Chapter 6 to 10

1 Confining yourself to Chapter 6, outline what we learn of Mr Loomis's background.

2 Show how, in Chapter 7, Robert O'Brien presents Ann's ambiguous attitude to Mr Loomis, wanting to like him yet feeling apprehensive and uncertain too.

3 What does Ann's vision of her wedding to Mr Loomis, and the form it will take, tell you about her?

4 Chapters 8 and 9 reveal fundamental differences in the characters of Ann and Mr Loomis. Describe these differences.

5 Describe the form Mr Loomis's illness takes up to the end of Chapter 10.

Chapter 11
June 4

The chapter begins with Ann's blunt admission that it has been a dreadful day. For one thing, Mr Loomis's temperature has reached at least one hundred and six degrees, and Ann believes he will die unless it falls soon. As Mr Loomis's illness reaches its climax he becomes thoroughly obsessed by Edward and terrified by his imagined presence. Although there has been every indication that he wishes to keep the story from Ann, he cannot control what he says in his delirious outbursts, and the whole appalling truth is revealed in stages throughout the day.

Ann decides that she cannot leave Mr Loomis alone while the nightmare persists which is yet a further constraint upon her. However, it means that she is present to learn the truth of who Edward is and what happened to him. The morning yields little information about Edward. Mr Loomis's belief that Edward is near the farm or actually inside the house has an unsettling effect upon Ann.

In an attempt to pacify Mr Loomis, she fetches the radiation suit from the wagon to show that no one has stolen it, but in the afternoon Mr Loomis lapses into yet another nightmare, again about Edward. This dream is a re-enactment of the crucial moments leading up to Edward's death. Ann, of course, can hear only Mr Loomis's side of the argument, although it is easy to deduce from this what Edward must have said. It allows her to piece together the fragments she has already heard into a story which is both gripping in its tension and disturbing in what it tells us about human nature under extreme stress.

Whereas in Chapter 6, Mr Loomis had given the impression that it was he alone who had been working in the laboratory when war started, Ann now learns that Edward had been present too. Mary and Billy, mentioned at the close of Chapter 7, are Edward's wife and child, about whose safety he is very worried. His dilemma is stark and without a solution. He wishes to leave the laboratory to discover if they are alive or dead. To enter a radioactive world he will have to wear the only radiation-proof suit of its kind in the world, leaving Mr Loomis to trust him to return. Mr Loomis, naturally but selfishly, cannot be so trusting; Edward, equally naturally and equally selfishly, cannot resist attempting to leave. Even to the end, Ann is unsure of what actually happened, but three patched-up bullet holes in the chest of the suit reveal to her that if Edward had been wearing the suit when the shots were fired then he is certainly dead.

When the worst of Mr Loomis's nightmare has passed and he seems too exhausted even to rise from bed, Ann leaves him and goes to church to pray for his recovery, and for strength to cope with what she has heard.

he thinks Edward is here . . . something vague and dreadful Mr Loomis's dreams about Edward take several forms. Those he has in the morning depict Edward as a kind of indestructable presence, forever haunting Mr Loomis. In the afternoon, the dream is of a different kind, dramatizing the actual events leading up to his shooting Edward.

'Thank you,' he said. 'That's good.' His clarity of thought lasts for seconds only before reality and fantasy intermingle in his mind. Such rapid changes naturally make it all the more difficult for Ann to look after him.

I will humour his dream . . . less worried Ann's well-meaning attempt at soothing him seems to backfire judging by what she says in the next paragraph.

I am glad it was only a dream . . . murder the other Notice Ann's unwitting irony here. Mr Loomis's dream is a re-creation of what happened, not a distortion of reality in the way that nightmares usually are.

I know how he felt Edward's worry for his family parallels Ann's for hers.

One suit, and two people These five simple words admirably convey the impossible position both men are in.

Poor Edward . . . why he would not An instance of Ann's ability to identify imaginatively with the feelings and needs of others, even someone she has never met. It is a faculty absent in Mr Loomis for much of the second half of the novel.

An idea came to me . . . do it anyway She is reluctant partly because her action seems to be a betrayal of trust in Mr Loomis and partly because she fears what she might find.

Even though he may be a murderer, I do not want him to die The

'may' is important. The evidence points to Mr Loomis having killed
Edward, but Ann is as yet reluctant to accept it.

Chapter 12
June 5–6

Mr Loomis survives the first night of the crisis of his illness but shows
no improvement the following morning. For the second night in
succession Ann has little sleep. Her exhaustion, together with her
worry over his chances of survival and the alarming story of Edward,
drive her to depression. She feels that she can do nothing to help him
and so goes to church, as much for her own benefit as for any help her
prayers might give him. Once there she finds a fledgling crow which
has fallen from its nest in the steeple. She places it in the grass outside
the church where its parents can find it. The incident cheers her a
little, for she superstitiously believes that birds are a good omen.

Mr Loomis's condition remains the same as the day passes. Ann
decides that even though she can do nothing medically to help him,
she can at least reassure him of her presence – and hope that he can
hear her. She reads him a poem, although she acknowledges that she
probably does it as much to soothe her own troubled mind as to bring
him comfort. It does seem to enable her to consider carefully the
implications of what happened between Edward and Mr Loomis.
Whereas she had seemed slightly unwilling at the end of Chapter 11 to
accept the possibility that Mr Loomis is a murderer, Ann does so now,
still with reluctance but with the realism which is so strong a part of
her character. She presents the case for each man systematically to
herself, but realizes that her ignorance of the characters of both men
makes it impossible to come to any certain moral conclusions. She
is even unsure whether she should tell Mr Loomis that she knows,
and yet she finds the prospect of keeping such a secret difficult to
imagine.

On the morning of June 6th, Mr Loomis still seems close to death
and Ann goes once more to church to pray for his recovery. On Ann's
return Mr Loomis's breathing is slower and deeper, but because she
knows nothing of the pattern radiation sickness takes she cannot be
sure whether this is a change for better or worse.

I recall from my high school course . . . This, together with other clues
  such as her love of books and her recollection from school that alcohol
  reduces fever, suggests that Ann was an attentive pupil at school. An
  American high school is rather like a British upper school, and takes pupils
  from 14 to 18.

I thought he might be stalking a spirit or an angel Ann is, of course, tired and depressed, but this helps confirm for the reader the strength of her belief in a world beyond this one.

cupola A rounded dome forming a roof.

two-by-four Planks of wood two inches thick and four inches wide.

I had forgotten to say any prayer at all Yet helping the fledgling crow is itself a kind of religious act for it suggests an instinctive faith in the future, and is a simple demonstration of one creature caring for another.

Gray's 'Elegy Written in a Country Churchyard' Written in 1750, it is one of the most famous poems in English.

From what he said in his dream . . . That was what he finally did In this long sequence, notice Ann's honesty to herself. She refuses to take the easy, self-deceiving course and try to convince herself that Mr Loomis was justified in shooting Edward, a tempting enough alternative given that it is Mr Loomis with whom she must live if he recovers.

The apple blossoms had wilted and fallen off A delicate symbolic image showing how Ann's dreams of an idyllic future with Mr Loomis have wilted also. Ann, remember, had associated apple blossom with marriage in Chapter 8.

Chapter 13
June 7–8

June 7th shows an improvement in Mr Loomis's health. He has survived the critical period of his illness and now seems likely to live. Ann's diary entry for June 7th is reflective in its tone. Her line of thought is worth following for it provides subtle contrasts between what she hopes for and what she actually has, between her aspirations and reality.

Caring for Mr Loomis has convinced Ann that she is unsuited to nursing. This leads her quite naturally to think of her ambition to become a teacher and the difficulty she has in accepting that she will never be one. This in turn leads her to think of her love of books and the pitiful supply she has at home. She becomes excited at the prospect of Mr Loomis using the safe-suit to bring her some books from Ogdentown. Her excitement is immediately qualified by thoughts that such books might still be radioactive and therefore dangerous. Her imagination quickly offers solutions to overcome this problem, only to suffer another reversal; Mr Loomis is not interested in books and might not want to go, and this leads Ann to the most momentous thought of all. Perhaps she could go, using the safe-suit. However, reality bursts upon her dream; she remembers Edward, and in doing so remembers that Mr Loomis has already killed to retain the safe-suit.

On June 8th, Mr Loomis opens his eyes for the first time and tries to speak to Ann, although he is still helplessly weak. On an impulse, Ann decides to move the stove from the barn into the kitchen using the tractor. She does so, and feels an immense sense of achievement.

I like books and reading more than anything else An important reminder here of Ann's need for the imaginative delight and personal enrichment which books give.

I would like to buy – would *have* liked to buy Ann's self-correction reminds us of her plight. It also indicates, too, that for the briefest of moments she had forgotten the circumstances of her situation.

Though he might not be . . . not much of a reader Notice how, within this passage, Robert O'Brien has subtly reinforced the different attitudes Ann and Mr Loomis have towards reading. It points to fundamental differences between them as people. For Mr Loomis, reading is a merely functional activity, a means of gathering information; for Ann, as we noted above, it is a source of deep personal satisfaction.

I could go. That is, if he would lend me the safe-suit As Ann realizes in the next sentence, what she proposes is alarmingly similar to what Edward had wanted.

Chapter 14
June 15

The events of this chapter cover the previous week without the subdivision into separate days which is a feature of her journal elsewhere. It begins on a note of high optimism. Ann celebrates her birthday and Mr Loomis is well enough to share a birthday supper with her. However, as she recounts the happenings of the previous week, we begin to wonder if her happiness is a little misplaced. The week begins encouragingly enough with a steady improvement in Mr Loomis's health.

Confident that he will recover, Ann now turns her mind to cultivating the garden and the field which she had neglected while nursing Mr Loomis. She realizes the importance of planting seed to gather new seeds for future harvests. Ann is aware of the seriousness of the problem, but is sure that she can deal with it. She does not intend to mention it to Mr Loomis. She discovers that he has been thinking of the same thing, though, and his words to her on the topic announce a fundamental change in their relationship.

From being acquiescent, he becomes aggressive in his questioning, interrupting Ann impatiently as she explains why the planting has not been finished, driving her without cause onto the defensive, making her feel guilty that she had gone to church to pray for him. When he becomes calmer, he explains that he worries about their food supply even to the extent of dreaming about it. This is understandable of course, but the different ways in which they have responded to the problem once again signal deep-rooted differences in their characters. Ann has been rational and level-headed, Mr Loomis nervous and suspicious. While Ann recognizes that, having survived his illness, he now considers the valley to be as much his as hers, she does not seem fully to realize that this will affect the balance of power between them – and not to her advantage.

A second, more trivial, incident also shows Mr Loomis asserting his individuality. Ann hears a crash from the bedroom and discovers Mr Loomis on the floor having tried to get up on his own. He fiercely refuses her offer of help, and drags himself unaided back to bed. In one respect this is quite natural. He is feeling better and the fact of being helpless and reliant on someone else annoys him. Still, his tone to Ann is scarcely justified, even though she is quick to record in her diary that she understands his embarrassment.

At the end of the chapter, Ann mentions that Mr Loomis's good humour is restored; we recall, too, the evident success of the celebration dinner mentioned at the beginning of the chapter, and Mr Loomis's appreciative response. But he has also displayed ingratitude, impatience and anger with Ann, asserting his own will against hers for the first time. His prickly behaviour makes the reader wonder just what Ann has in store for herself.

I wanted to hug him Ann is overjoyed partly because his words are effectively the only contact she has had with Mr Loomis since his illness became critical, and partly because they confirm that her idea of playing the piano for him was a good and beneficial one. Notice, too, the warmth of Ann's feelings for Mr Loomis, something which contrasts throughout the novel with his for her.

In any case it was not as bad as it might have been Unlike Mr Loomis, Ann has the opportunity to inspect the garden and reassure herself. She has, also, invaluable experience of farming and the cultivation of crops, something of which Mr Loomis knows comparatively little.

The first one I could almost call a scolding Mr Loomis's concern is quite understandable. He is ignorant of farming and fear feeds on ignorance. What is disturbing, however, is the tone of voice he assumes, and his incredulity when Ann tells him she has visited the church three times. Their differing attitudes to the church point to the same differences in character as their different attitudes to reading. There is a spiritual dimension to Ann which is lacking in Mr Loomis.

I even dream about it Mr Loomis's worry about maintaining an adequate food supply borders on the obsessive.

And now he considered the valley . . . used to the idea Ann recognizes the change in his attitude without being fully aware of the possible consequences.

Chapter 15
June 22

This is a very important chapter in the relationship between Ann and Mr Loomis, for the anxiety which was awakened in the reader's mind by Mr Loomis's behaviour in the previous chapter begins to be shared by Ann herself in this one. His efforts to teach himself to walk exclude her totally, and show a lack of the generosity which is so prominent a feature of Ann's character. She is puzzled by his secrecy, attributing it to embarrassment or his wish to surprise her. But the two important qualifying words 'probably' and 'maybe' reveal her real ignorance of his motive; they express what she hopes rather than what she knows. This feeling of exclusion is emphasized when, on June 19th, she hears his footsteps and wants to run into his bedroom and congratulate him, but has to restrain herself.

The subsequent conversation she has with Mr Loomis does little to indicate that there is any warmth of feeling for her on his part. There are no words of thanks to her for caring for him. Instead, he questions her curtly on the distance to Ogdentown, shows little understanding of her need for novels and plays to read, and becomes angry when she is rash enough to mention borrowing the safety-suit. Even when he becomes a little less unfriendly and explains why the suit is so important, his tone does not soften, but remains formal and distant. Ann recognizes that she is in the same predicament as Edward had been. Any mention of her borrowing the suit will anger Mr Loomis, so she does not pursue the matter.

There is further cause for concern when Mr Loomis questions her closely about the crops she has planted. In fact it is not so much a questioning as an interrogation. There is no doubt that he is right in his belief that beets and wheat must be grown in order to save the seed for future years. What is so disturbing is his relentless single-mindedness. In an important paragraph – the seventh from the end of the chapter – Ann recognizes that Mr Loomis's wish to keep the valley alive is not dissimilar to the one she had in Chapter 9; yet she feels uneasy about it without knowing why. The reader has perhaps begun to suspect that it is because any future will be shaped according to Mr Loomis's view, not Ann's.

He looked up without expression and said, 'It's something I have to do.' The lack of expression on his face when Ann asks him what is clearly a question inviting him to talk, together with the brevity of his reply, show his lack of interest in her as a person. This attitude had been hinted at in the previous chapter, but is more strongly implied here.

'No,' he said ... 'Never touch it.' Note how the angry, commanding tone is conveyed through the shortness of the sentences.

The idea of taking it to get some novels – it's too foolish to consider Everything that Mr Loomis says about the importance of the suit is true, and he is probably right to regard a trip to a library as an unnecessary risk. Ann concedes that he is. Even so, one wonders if there are any circumstances at all under which he would allow Ann to wear the suit and leave the valley. We remember that he would not allow Edward to use the suit to seek his family. Mr Loomis's attitude here is perfectly sensible, but we suspect that the reason he gives Ann is not the real one. It is a rational explanation which diverts attention from the real reason – his terror of being stranded without the suit.

And on the back porch, too, where I can see the planting The sinister significance of this instruction becomes apparent in the next chapter.

But it was true ... counted on the tractor Once more Ann concedes that Mr Loomis is right – another indication of the shift in the balance of power within the relationship.

Revision questions on Chapters 11 to 15

1 Using material from Chapter 11, give a brief outline of what happens in Mr Loomis's nightmare. What effect does it seem to have upon him?

2 What do we learn of Ann from the way she responds to Mr Loomis's dream in Chapter 12?

3 Ann begins Chapter 14 by saying that the past week has been one of the best. What evidence is there in the Chapter to make the reader feel less optimistic?

4 Outline the differences in character which begin to emerge between Ann and Mr Loomis in Chapter 15.

Chapter 16
June 24

Mr Loomis's behaviour in the few days leading up to this entry in Ann's journal gives her cause for concern, and marks a considerable deterioration in their relationship which reaches a minor crisis on June 23rd. The tension in the novel rises as a consequence. Mr Loomis observes Ann while she works, in the way that a master would watch a slave. This gives vital confirmation of the way in which he regards her as being a mere functionary rather than a human being. His callousness is further revealed that evening when Ann tries to engage him in conversation. She realizes that she knows very little about him and finds him difficult to understand. She has even formulated a theory to explain his reluctance to speak about the past; the horrible events of the past months have obliterated any memory of what his life was like before the war.

Her efforts fail dismally. In answer to Ann's questions he offers only the briefest of replies and then gives only a list of impersonal educational and career details. Nothing of his personality emerges. When Ann probes a little deeper he reacts violently. His sudden violence frightens Ann, who accidentally strikes him while trying to retain her balance. Mr Loomis's remarks that she should not have hit him are chilling in their quietness. Significantly, Ann apologizes even though the blow was unintentional. It is significant for it is a tacit display of weakness on Ann's part, and provides further evidence that Mr Loomis is now the dominating partner in their relationship.

While she prepares supper, Ann attempts to rationalize Mr Loomis's behaviour by trying to convince herself that he was only making a 'pass' at her. But Ann is far too sensible to be deluded by such a belief no matter how consoling it would be to accept it. She recognizes that when Mr Loomis seized her he was taking hold of a possession. Although she cannot explain clearly what she feels, it is evident that she understands its essence. She is no longer even a junior partner in their relationship, but merely an object to be used. The chapter ends on an uneasy note. Mr Loomis's growing strength, instead of bringing joy, now brings danger, for when he is restored to full mobility the threat he presents to Ann will be even greater.

rather like an overseer An overseer was the person on a plantation responsible for superintending the slaves. Notice the ironic reversal of roles here. Hitherto, Ann watched over Mr Loomis during his illness; now he watches over her, but for a far more sinister reason.

He never talked about himself . . . playing the piano Like Ann, we cannot know the reasons for Mr Loomis's reticence and his apparent lack of interest in her.

When he thought back . . . about the past It is natural that Ann should have evolved this theory for, as we will see in the note below, the blotting out of the past is something which she has had to do herself. In other words, she believes that his way of coping with the past parallels hers.

Nyack A small town in the south-east of New York state.

in a naval ordnance laboratory Mr Loomis had never been to sea. He spent his time in the navy working on the development of guns for warships.

chemistry major Mr Loomis has specialized in the study of chemistry at university.

'I thought you were coming to that' This is the second time that Mr Loomis has guessed Ann's thoughts. The first occurred near the end of the previous chapter when he told Ann that he knew what she was thinking. It emphasizes that being older and more experienced than Ann gives Mr Loomis yet another advantage over her.

There was nothing gentle . . . at *The Farm Mechanic* A further example of the way in which he regards Ann as an object rather than as a person.

'Interested in what?' . . . further off balance Like Ann, the reader has no means of knowing why the topic of marriage provokes such a violent response from Mr Loomis.

In a very quiet voice The quietness of Mr Loomis's voice when he threatens Ann suggests the self-controlled suppression of great anger, which is even more sinister than if he had lost his temper and raged at her.

I put the thought out of my head A glimpse of the great strength of mind it has taken for Ann to come to terms with the loss of everyone dear to her. Her momentary yearning for her family also draws attention to her present vulnerability.

Chapter 17
June 30

Chapter 17 begins a long and detailed entry embracing the next two chapters as well which together cover the dramatic breakdown of the relationship between Ann and Mr Loomis. It opens with the startling announcement that Ann is once again living in the cave, having moved there on June 28th, and goes on to explain the events leading up to her decision to move.

Ann spends the day after Mr Loomis's pass at her, June 25th, working hard on the farm. She feels strained and worried. Although the duties she performs are part of a constant, everyday routine they bring her little reassurance; she is uncomfortably aware that her life has changed.

At dinner that evening, Mr Loomis appears to have undergone a change of heart. He announces that as he is feeling stronger he can now eat in the dining-room, and during the meal makes an effort to engage Ann in conversation, even complimenting her. Ann relaxes, which is precisely what he intends, for the rest of the chapter makes plain that he has devised a calculated and cruel strategy to make her aware of his power over her. His behaviour at dinner is merely a means of lowering her defences, the opening move of his plan.

On the surface Mr Loomis's request that Ann reads to him appears perfectly reasonable and civilized. But the apparent reasonableness hides a much more unpleasant reality. Ann is reluctant to do it, partly because she is tired, but also because she senses that there is a hidden motive in what he asks. She does not want to read to him but does not know how to refuse, which she suspects is something that he knows.

Without any overt suggestion of threat, he can make her do as he wishes, all under the guise of a quaint and comforting pastime, a family reading.

After the first half-hour Ann is aware that he is no longer even listening to her, yet exhausted though she is she continues to read. In doing so she proclaims Mr Loomis's victory over her. Although it makes her both nervous and afraid, she attempts to convince herself that perhaps Mr Loomis's request was innocent enough; that he merely found the sound of her voice soothing.

hopper A large cone-shaped machine which holds the fertilizer and releases it gradually into the spreader.

I heard a chair scrape . . . 'I am still weak, but not sick.' Note the way in which Mr Loomis informs Ann of his decision. He does not consult her or even go to the kitchen door to tell her that he feels well enough to eat in the dining-room. Instead, he sits at the table and presents her with a *fait accompli*. Implicit in what he says and does here is his idea that he dominates.

He had even lighted two lamps Ready for Ann to read to him, and further evidence that his request is part of a preconceived plan.

Pride and Prejudice by Jane Austen First published in 1813, *Pride and Prejudice* is perhaps Jane Austen's most popular novel. Its main characters, Elizabeth Bennet and Mr Darcy, begin by disliking each other, but eventually fall in love and marry.

Meanwhile if I could help him I should Another example of Ann's moral seriousness.

Chapter 18
Still June 30

Mr Loomis's devious scheme to assert his own power by frightening Ann continues in this chapter. The night after he had asked her to read to him (the 26th), he asks her to play the piano. Once again, the request seems perfectly unexceptional, and it is deadly just because of this. With great skill he has selected two of Ann's favourite diversions to use in his campaign against her. This means that she cannot accuse him of forcing her to do things she does not like. The terror he creates in her mind is achieved much more subtly than this and consists in generating acute mental uncertainty. Two examples will show his skill as a tormentor. Firstly, she has to sit with her back to him in order to play the piano. Of itself there is nothing sinister in this, except that her fear of him generated in the last chapter is fuelled here when she has to sit where she cannot see him but where he can see her. That seems to be his motive in asking for music; it is a further tactic in his cruel, and puzzling, campaign against her.

The second example occurs when she is actually playing. As she is nervous, she plays badly which of course informs Mr Loomis that his campaign of subtle terror is working. When she rallies and plays an easier piece well, the noise of his stick on the floor makes her spin round as she thinks he is coming for her. Yet he passes the incident off with an excuse. The result is as he wishes. Ann's fragile composure cracks. She suspects, doubtless correctly, that he tapped the floor deliberately in order to frighten her, yet she cannot be absolutely sure.

The crisis comes the following night, June 27th. Mr Loomis does not ask Ann to read or play to him, but retires to his room immediately after dinner. Ann walks to the church and enjoys the tranquillity of the scene which contrasts strongly with the tension in the house. On her way back, she sees Mr Loomis leave the house and walk, without a stick. Feeling uneasy, she goes to bed, but is awoken by Faro's growling. She realizes with horror that Mr Loomis is in her room. His purpose is clear, he has come to rape her. After a desperate struggle Ann manages to escape.

in my father's chair Notice how effectively this image shows Mr Loomis gradually taking control of the house. That he should be implementing his plan to terrorize her from the chair in which her father once sat is, of course, ironic.

Clementi Sonatina Clementi was an Italian composer who lived from 1752 to 1832. A sonatina is a short simple piece of music written usually for the piano.

***Andante* by Heller** Andante is a musical instruction that the piece should be played slowly and distinctly. Heller was an Hungarian composer who lived from 1813 to 1888.

'Tired so soon?' he said His tone feigns concern, but is both mocking and callous.

maybe he is trying to frighten me. But why should he? Despite all that has happened, Ann is still reluctant to believe the worst of Mr Loomis.

I was a little surprised . . . I had said I was tired Once more, Ann shows her youth and inexperience in assessing Mr Loomis's behaviour.

whippoorwills Whip-poor-wills are American birds rather like swifts. Their name mimics their cry.

fireflies Winged insects which give off a phosphorescent light.

(I stayed still) Ann remains hidden from Mr Loomis, a telling indication of her uneasiness.

He definitely did not have the cane The implication of this is that Mr Loomis has been misleading Ann into thinking he is weaker than he actually is.

He crept forward . . . felt or imagined Mr Loomis abandons his subtle, mental cruelty to Ann for a violent, physical attack. It is a horrifying example of his callous, uncaring attitude towards her.

His grip . . . the smooth floor Mr Loomis is like some savage predatory animal dragging his prey toward him.

Chapter 19
June 30 (continued)

More frightened than she has ever been in her life, Ann flees the house. She stops at the store, too terrified at first even to think. Eventually, she regains a little composure and realizes that after what has happened, it is possible that she will never enter her house again, at least not as long as Mr Loomis is there. She decides to gather some essentials from the store and take them to the cave. Once there, she watches all night, even though she is certain that Mr Loomis does not know about the cave, and even if he did he would not be strong enough to walk there. Her night-long vigil is a measure of extreme caution prompted by extreme fear.

The next morning she sees that Faro is tracking her to the store. More ominously, she sees Mr Loomis watching Faro to try to discover which path she took. Ann thanks her good luck that she had not fled straight to the cave, for the store is out of sight of the house and she is confident that Mr Loomis will not be able to follow Faro's movements.

When Faro arrives, Ann makes what proves to be a grave mistake. She is so intent on watching the house that she forgets to feed him. Faro returns to the house, and Ann watches as Mr Loomis feeds him and then fastens him up. The implication of this is clear: he intends to use Faro to track down Ann.

As she watches Mr Loomis's movements, Ann begins to think of the future. She decides that some kind of compromise must be reached between herself and Mr Loomis, one in which they both share the valley but live separate lives. Of course, Ann is too much of a realist to believe that this is a likely possibility, but her common sense tells her that at least the effort must be made. Accordingly, she decides that she must talk to Mr Loomis.

I have never been so afraid This simple statement conveys not only the extent of Ann's fear, but the desperate nature of her situation. She has literally no one to turn to. The comment which closes her entry for May 21st (page 9), that there are worse things than being alone, proves to be uncomfortably true.

a small, chill wind had blown up The dramatic use Robert O'Brien makes of this wind provides a good example of his economical technique as a writer. Firstly, the wind makes Ann feel cold. This has the double effect of emphasizing her vulnerability and increasing our sympathy for her. But there is more than this for it is used to create a moment of dramatic suspense. A little later, when she hears the store door shut with a thud, she is terrified that it is Mr Loomis. She listens in agonized fear before realizing that it is only the wind.

I could not let him starve An important example of Ann's compassion which can be contrasted with Mr Loomis's cruel treatment of her.

Chapter 20
July 1

On June 30th, Ann receives confirmation that Mr Loomis plans to use Faro to track her down. As yet, though, he does not have the strength to implement his plan fully, so he engages in a variation of the subtle terror-raising tactics he had used before he tried to rape her. Hoping that Ann is watching his every movement, he follows Faro, keeping him on the leash. Mr Loomis's purpose is clear. He is giving Ann warning of what he intends and hopes that the prospect will demoralize her. Ann likens her predicament to a chess game. She is an unwilling player in a game which only her opponent can win.

Before finally going into the house for the evening, Mr Loomis provides another example of his uncanny ability to wage an unsettling war of nerves. He ties up Faro, returns to the road and then allows his gaze to sweep the entire valley. As he stares in Ann's direction she is so jumpy that she almost puts down her binoculars and hides in the cave. This is exactly the response Mr Loomis would wish for. Coming immediately after he has tied up Faro, his inspection of the valley is a symbolic gesture, designed to tell Ann that he will find her wherever she is. Ann herself spends the evening building a concealed fireplace so that the flames of her cooking fire will not be visible from the house.

On the morning of July 1st, she sets out for the house to discuss with Mr Loomis how they will arrange their lives in future. She is astonished when he seems both apologetic and, when she tells him she will not return to the house, concerned as to where she will live. Yet Ann is not deceived by his apparent remorse. She briskly makes arrangements with him, suspecting all the while that he is not being entirely open with her. The absence of Faro puzzles her, leading her to believe that the dog has been tied up in the house. This in turn puts a frightening idea into her mind: perhaps Mr Loomis intends to enslave Ann in the same way. She is alarmingly close to the truth.

For the rest of the day, Ann attends to the crops and the cow, and brings Mr Loomis groceries from the store. By late afternoon, having finished her work and successfully negotiated a day under her new régime, she feels a little happier. However, back at the cave, she watches as Mr Loomis brings out Faro and takes him to the back of the house to the garden where Ann had worked. She realizes that he is checking whether the dog actually was tracking her on the road to the store. Satisfied with the result, Mr Loomis secures Faro once more and then starts the tractor, driving it round the yard before returning it to the barn. His reason for doing so is to become evident soon.

At dusk, Ann lights her fire and checks that it cannot be seen from the direction of the house. She ponders on her predicament, regretting that Mr Loomis ever came to the valley. Her thoughts lead to speculation on the possibility of life surviving elsewhere. Had Mr Loomis taken another road he might have found other survivors, and never troubled Ann at all. Structurally, the final three paragraphs of the chapter serve to provide cohesion. Ann's understanding that loneliness is preferable to tyranny takes the reader back to the opening chapter of the book where she expresses a similar idea. Her speculations on the possibility of life surviving elsewhere, given their longest treatment here, point forward to the conclusion of the book.

kerosene An inflammable oil made from coal or petroleum.
'Where will you stay?' The first of Mr Loomis's questions in which a desire to find out where she is staying masquerades as concern for her welfare.
But I knew it was not true Ann is no longer willing to give Mr Loomis the benefit of the doubt.
I need to stay alive . . . If we are to stay alive A revealing piece of dialogue. Notice that on both occasions Ann includes Mr Loomis – 'you' and 'we'. He betrays his selfish intention by his use of 'I'. Ann is important to him only insofar as she can help him stay alive.
burlap Coarse canvas.

Revision questions on Chapters 16 to 20

1 What evidence is there in Chapter 16 that Ann is in considerable danger from Mr Loomis?

2 Look carefully at Chapters 18 and 19 and describe the way in which Mr Loomis quite deliberately seeks to tyrannize Ann.

3 What aspects of Mr Loomis's character are revealed in his conversation with Ann in Chapter 20?

4 Why are Ann's thoughts, as expressed in the final three paragraphs of Chapter 20, important to the structure of the novel?

Chapter 21
August 4 (I think)

In the month between this entry and the last one, Ann's life has become more desperate than she could possibly have imagined. The opening paragraph briefly sketches the circumstances under which she is living, more like a hunted animal than a human being. Having shown us this further deterioration in her life, she begins the account of events leading up to it.

For some ten days after the attempted rape, she followed her system of working on the farm in the daytime and returning to the cave at night. She sees little of Mr Loomis. Although she would like to believe that he has accepted the new system and will leave her alone, she cannot so delude herself. He is, in fact, planning and biding his time. On one occasion he races the tractor at top speed towards Burden Hill, a seemingly pointless exercise which in fact is all part of a larger plan he is developing. On another occasion, he spies on Ann from the edge of Burden Creek to try to discover where she comes from. She outwits him and wins a minor victory, only to make a serious error a little later.

It begins when she decides to kill a chicken and wishes to return to the cave for a knife and the milk pail she had forgotten. Using the pretext of filling Mr Loomis's water can in the stream, she runs back to the cave to collect the tools. Her mistake becomes apparent in a conversation she has with Mr Loomis. She discovers that he has taken possession of the key to the tractor, and as she wishes to spread fertilizer on the wheat decides to ask him for it. His manner is a curious mixture of pleasantness and threat. He tells Ann that he will think about letting her have the key, yet another example of his deeply possessive nature. Just as he is about to step back inside the house, he lets Ann know that he saw her go to the pond with his water can and return with her knife and milk pail as well. Ann is baffled and annoyed at herself, for although Mr Loomis still does not know the exact location of her hideout, her carelessness means that he knows it is merely a few minutes from the pond.

The incident is important for it shows how a minor slip can have grave consequences in the unrelenting battle which is being waged with Mr Loomis. Both Ann and he constantly watch each other's movements and behaviour, and ponder the significance of what they see. Ann, for example, realizes that Mr Loomis has removed the ignition key from the tractor because he thinks that she might steal it. She sees it as part of a larger pattern of behaviour. Everything which might be of use to her – the safe-suit, Faro, and now the tractor – is taken away from her.

Unable to do the work she intended, Ann walks to the store, gathers some more provisions, including fishing tackle, and makes her way back to the cave. She spends the rest of the day fishing.

Once or twice I stopped off at the church . . . odd times during the day Ann's continued churchgoing after the war seems partly because of a need to feel that there are rituals and customs which are timeless. As such, they offer a much-needed spiritual link with the past and a brief, though consoling, feeling of normality. Now, driven from her home, she has been estranged from any vestige of normal life with which she associates the church.

Burden Hill A timely reminder, together with the mention of Burden Creek a little later, of the close and long association Ann's family have had with the valley. It makes the precarious, dispossessed life she leads at present even more unfair.

where there were trees and bushes . . . if I could tell what he was up to Ann spies on Mr Loomis as he prepares to spy on her. The incident sums up neatly the close surveillance under which they keep each other.

I passed just above the crabapple tree . . . thickly on the branches The reader recalls that morning in early summer when Ann's thoughts of having apple blossom at her wedding lead to her thoughts of marriage to Mr Loomis. The mention of the apples hanging thickly on the branches has another symbolic function. The blossom on the tree has, in the natural course of events, given way to fruit. Ann's thoughts of marriage, associated in our mind with the blossom, have been blighted.

divided it evenly into two piles, one for him, one for me Ann's scrupulous fairness in her treatment of Mr Loomis is remarkable, and offers further evidence of her strictly honest, morally admirable character. It does, of course, put her at a distinct disadvantage against someone as devious as Mr Loomis.

His legs were getting back to normal Every mention of Mr Loomis's return to strength marks an increase in the danger Ann faces.

'Possibly I will fertilize the wheat myself.' A sign of his improving health and growing independence. Ironically, by bringing him food and water, Ann is helping him reach that state of health where he can tyrannize her more successfully.

As he was going in he said With admirably malicious timing, Mr Loomis leaves his most disconcerting comment until just before he closes the door on Ann.

Chapter 22
August 4 (continued)

After the many events described in the previous chapter, this one is shorter, and the action is interspersed with Ann's recollection of a visit she made to the Kleins' living quarters above the store, and possible reasons why Mr Loomis might be carrying a gun. The action concentrates on two principal episodes.

The first begins when Ann scrupulously divides the fish she has caught in half and leaves Mr Loomis's share at his door. On her way back to the store she suddenly sees him driving the tractor in her direction. She hides and watches as he passes, holding a rifle in his hand. She is puzzled by his seemingly odd behaviour, stopping the tractor a hundred feet from the store and approaching cautiously on foot, but when his face appears at the window of the Kleins' living-quarters, his purpose becomes clear. He believed that Ann was using it as her hideaway and by mounting a surprise attack presumably hoped to recapture her. His decision to carry a gun worries Ann, but she deduces that his intention is not to shoot her but to discourage her from shooting at him. If she is right, then his behaviour is prompted at least in part by wariness of the threat he feels she poses to him.

The second, and briefer, episode involves Mr Loomis padlocking both doors to the store before he drives off.

I placed his share, one and a half fish Notice once again how attention is drawn to Ann's sense of fairness, which contrasts so vividly with the closely possessive, suspicious behaviour of Mr Loomis.

He looked like an Indian on horseback in an old Western movie In less sombre circumstances the image of a grown man 'riding' a tractor and waving a rifle would be rather comic.

There was a pattern that kept repeating The pattern seems to be that it is fear which governs Mr Loomis's behaviour, making him thoroughly self-centred.

to go into the store . . . permission each time Another feature of the pattern. Mr Loomis is gradually removing those facilities which make it possible for Ann to live any kind of independent life.

Chapter 23
August 4 (continued)

This chapter completes the cycle of events begun in Chapter 21 and shows the dire situation Ann is in. On the morning after Mr Loomis had padlocked the store doors, Ann considers his possible reasons for doing so. She hopes that it is merely another example of his acute wish to ration precious provisions. Eager to believe that there is nothing more sinister to it than this, her mind readily provides other instances of the same characteristic. Yet once again, she is too sensible to discount the alarming alternative: that he intends starving her into submission. She decides that she must find out, and accordingly approaches the house to ask for the key to the store. Mr Loomis shoots at her and Ann flees for shelter. While dressing her wounded ankle and thinking of the reasons for this drastic change in Mr Loomis's tactics, she realizes the awful truth: Mr Loomis intended to maim her only and then catch her. Ann is thoroughly bewildered by his behaviour.

She has little time for reflection, however, for the nightmare continues. The sound of the tractor alerts her to the fact that Mr Loomis is anxious to pursue his advantage. On reaching the store, he dismounts and, with Faro, picks up the scent of her morning route to the farm. Mr Loomis is in no hurry, but the tension of the chapter develops inexorably as Faro leads him towards the cave. Ann hastily collects some belongings and abandons her makeshift home. While she waits, ready to run again if necessary, she realizes that she must shoot Faro; it is the only chance she has of escape. Yet, despite the danger that the dog poses to her liberty, she cannot do it.

Within minutes they are at the cave, and Ann smells smoke. When it is safe she investigates the damage, and discovers that Mr Loomis has burnt whatever he can, destroyed her fire-wall and removed almost everything else. Ann feels demoralized. Physically injured from the wound in her leg, she is spiritually wounded, too, when she surveys the charred remains of her few possessions. Yet, remarkably, the worst part of the nightmare for her is not that she has been shot at, or even that she has been driven from the cave, but that at one point she decided to kill Faro.

I knew that he had a compulsion . . . was all it meant Ann is trying to convince herself that there is a perfectly normal explanation from the pattern of Mr Loomis's behaviour, to the extent that she is willing to demean her own ability to take a long-term view. She perceives the pattern quite correctly but attributes the wrong cause to it. Mr Loomis's concern with rationing does not spring from a reasonable and quite justifiable need for conversation but from a fanatical and selfish desire for his own survival regardless of any cost to Ann.

There was little point in wondering. I had to find out Another example of Ann's decisiveness.

perhaps, in a way, these new things . . . made me feel better Once more Ann generously thinks the best rather than the worst of Mr Loomis. Her moderate and considerate idea contrasts bleakly with his behaviour towards her a moment or two later.

It was, in fact, time to bring him some more stores anyway Ann has forgotten that Mr Loomis no longer needs her to bring him provisions. He can drive the tractor to the store until he is strong enough to walk there.

I am sitting beside the pond . . . Note that Ann moves into the present

tense to describe the dreadful account of Mr Loomis tracking her with
Faro. This makes it more vivid in the reader's mind.

why must he do it? She can provide no answer. As a reasonable person
who wished for nothing more than to live in harmony with Mr Loomis,
Ann finds his inhuman behaviour quite incomprehensible.

draw the bead Ann lines up her target in the sights of her rifle.

I cannot do it Logic has told Ann that she must kill Faro. Her love for him
(perhaps, too, her memory that he is her last living link with her family)
prevents her.

It is hard to keep from crying again . . . no signs of them in the fire
Mr Loomis's destruction of her possessions is yet another step in his
systematic plan to prevent her from living independently. Notice, too, that
whereas Ann shared the food equally between them, Mr Loomis removes
her last few remaining tins from the cave.

It makes me feel as much a murderer as Mr Loomis For Ann the
intention to murder is as grave as the act itself. This comment offers an
insight into the strict code of morality by which she conducts her life.

Chapter 24
August 6

Despite having lived for a month with only a hollow tree for shelter
and the simplest of food to sustain her, Ann begins this entry in good
heart having decided to steal the safe-suit and leave the valley. The
decision to act, after a period of weakness and uncertainty, buoys up
her spirit, and the circumstances leading to it are important. Mr
Loomis, unaware that Ann is ill and could be easily caught, leaves her
alone, confident that with Faro he can catch her when he wishes. Ann
sleeps a great deal and has a recurring dream, the most important one
of her life. It is a dream of another place, presumably to the south of
her valley, where she can live and where she is needed to teach
children to read.

She is aware of the danger involved in attempting to steal the
safe-suit, but believing that Mr Loomis is mad and that any recon-
ciliation is impossible she feels she has no other choice. Furthermore,
she wishes to hurt Mr Loomis, to gain revenge on him, and depriving
him of the suit will be the surest way of achieving this aim. So she will
satisfy two needs with one action. Her reason for wishing for revenge
is curious and very revealing. It has nothing to do with the two nights
when he virtually forced her to read and to play the piano to him; nor
with the attempted rape; nor with his shooting at her. It is because he
burnt her favourite book of short stories at the cave. Its loss and the
calculated philistinism which led Mr Loomis to destroy it motivate
Ann to the uncharacteristic desire for revenge.

It is Mr Loomis who unwittingly sets in motion the events which lead to the theft of his suit when he sets a simple trap to capture Ann. One afternoon Ann notices that the door to Klein's store is open. As time passes and there is no sign of Mr Loomis, she convinces herself, driven by her hunger, that he has forgotten to lock it. She approaches it cautiously but is shot at from the store window. Mr Loomis is determined to catch her this time, and pursues her with Faro. Ann realizes the need for extreme action, and thinks with remarkable clarity under stress. Collecting her gun from the tree, she cleverly doubles back and waits in hiding. Mr Loomis tries to stop Faro from leaping into the contaminated Burden Creek but releases the dog when Ann fires her rifle. It takes Faro five minutes to swim the creek in water which, we remember, is highly radioactive. By the following evening he is dead. According to her own views, expressed at the close of the previous chapter, Ann is now a murderer in deed as well as intention.

She now plans to take the suit the following day, soberly recording that this might be her last entry, for if she is caught attempting to steal the suit Mr Loomis will try to kill her. The chapter closes with her poignant memory of the joy she felt when ploughing the field, that occasion mentioned in Chapter 9 when she was so happy that she felt like singing.

Yet this dream was more important . . . waiting for a long time Is Ann's recurring dream a vision of another place which really exists or the expression of a deep-seated psychological desire? There is no way of telling, but the subject of the dream certainly coincides with two of Ann's deepest character traits: her wish to be socially useful, and her ambition to be an English teacher.

Was it so unrealistic . . . afraid to leave? Notice that this crucial idea has been burgeoning in Ann's mind since the end of Chapter 20. It is not suddenly sprung upon the reader here.

That memory stirred my harshest feelings towards Mr Loomis Even here Ann stops short of actually expressing hatred.

I could not bring myself to set the plan in motion This is unusual in Ann, who prefers activity to the agony of inactive uncertainty. Her hesitancy is a measure of the gravity of the plan.

it was he who set the plan in motion, without knowing what he was doing How Mr Loomis does this is explained in the next chapter.

I knew what I had to do This short sentence admirably expresses the speed and decisiveness of Ann's thought. The entire episode dealing with the way in which she quickly conceives her plan and puts it faultlessly into action demonstrates her resourcefulness and clear-headedness.

Chapter 25
August 7

The chapter begins with Ann having stolen the safe-suit and the wagon. Her plan has been so successful that it would be possible for her to leave the valley immediately. Yet she cannot leave without explaining herself to Mr Loomis. As she waits for him, she writes her penultimate entry.

She realizes that because Mr Loomis knows she is armed, he will be afraid to show himself. This is what she meant in the entry for August 6th when she wrote that Mr Loomis unwittingly set her plan in action. The fright she gave him when she fired into the air gave her the initiative. Now she must press it home.

Her plan is a simple one and is designed to take advantage of the fear that Mr Loomis has of her. Before daybreak she leaves him a note offering to meet him, unarmed, at the south end of the valley. It is an appointment she has no intention of keeping. Despite her doubts, the plan succeeds completely, allowing her to take possession of the wagon and the safe-suit while he is away. As she pulls the wagon past objects she has known for her entire life – the house, the swing, the treehouse – her mind fills with memories which serve to emphasize the enormity of her decision to leave the only home she has ever known. She thinks, too, of Mr Loomis, and realizes that she cannot leave without speaking to him even though at best he will speak discouragingly of her chances of finding other survivors, and at worst will try to kill her. So, wearing the safe-suit, she rolls the wagon into the deadness towards Ogdentown, returns to the valley and awaits Mr Loomis. The entry closes dramatically with Mr Loomis approaching on the tractor.

my father and I would sit at the kitchen table playing chess Ann has already referred to the game of chess early in Chapter 20 when she says that Mr Loomis's calculated plans against her are rather like those of a chess player. She felt then that she was in a game which only her opponent could win. The image reappears here. Just as her father usually beat her at chess, so Mr Loomis has the advantage against her in his 'game'. However, she sometimes beat her father by 'taking the offensive', and she employs precisely the same tactic now.

The note said this This is the first indication of what Ann's plan is. By having it unfold slowly in this way, Robert O'Brien cleverly builds up the suspense.

Tomorrow I will watch it from a strange place One of several sentences in the chapter designed to impress upon the reader, and Ann herself, the enormity of what she is doing. Two others are 'In a short time . . . depend on them' and 'His may be the last human voice . . .'

yet there was something inside me that resisted the idea Ann's reluctance to leave the valley secretly is entirely consistent with her character. It suggests both cowardice and duplicity, neither of which is a natural aspect of her personality.

Chapter 26
August 8

Mr Loomis, oblivious to everything, drives straight past where Ann is hiding, right to the top of Burden Hill from which he anxiously scans the road to Ogdentown. When she challenges him to drop his rifle, he is so overwrought that he turns and fires even though he cannot see her. Ann believes that he intends to kill, and rises from hiding quite certain that she faces death. It is her mention of Edward's fate which seems to save her, for the impact it has upon Mr Loomis is startling. He is unaware that Ann knew. The depth of his shock is apparent as much by his physical behaviour as by what he says: he lowers the rifle and steps back, almost as though he has been hit. Then he actually turns away from Ann, seemingly overcome with emotion, as if ashamed of himself. When she gives him her reasons for leaving, he pleads with her to stay.

His recent callous behaviour is put into perspective here, for we see not an evil man, but a man who is thoroughly frightened and whose fear has made him deranged. The moral initiative clearly lies with Ann in their conversation. Mr Loomis crumbles before her as she controls her fear and grows in self-assurance. But it is a precarious self-control, and her final words to him, as she admits, are childish. She secures her mask and steps into the deadness beyond the valley, expecting every moment to feel the pain of a bullet. Instead, Mr Loomis calls to her. Eventually, she understands his message. He is advising her to travel west, for before he entered the valley, he had seen birds circling in that direction, although he did not find out where.

Ann's journal closes when she awakens to a new morning of a new life. On the night of August 7th, her first in a dead land, she dreamed once more of the schoolroom and the children. She feels an inner certainty. Confident of the direction she must take, Ann Burden begins her quest filled with what is perhaps the most sustaining human emotion – hope.

'No,' he said, 'you don't know that . . .' Mr Loomis's words here, together with Ann's comment that his voice is weak, suggest that he is burdened by an enormous sense of guilt.

you have food. You have the tractor . . . So my last words were childish As Ann lists all of the things Mr Loomis has – food, the tractor, the store, the valley – she realizes the comparative security of Mr Loomis's future against her own. It is perhaps this which drives her nearly to tears and accounts for her immature, though true, criticism.

he was calling my name An important detail. Mr Loomis has called to Ann by name on only one other occasion – in Chapter 10 (page 80). That he does so now is a gesture of his understanding of her need to leave the valley.

I am hopeful The novel ends on a quiet and yet confident note.

Revision questions on Chapters 21 to 26

1 What evidence is there in Chapter 21 that Mr Loomis tries to keep Ann under close surveillance?

2 What part does locking the store play in Mr Loomis's plans?

3 Describe Ann's reactions to be being tracked by Faro and Mr Loomis in Chapter 23 and to having her possessions burnt.

4 Why is Ann's dream of the other valley and the children in the classroom so important to her?

5 Try to account for Mr Loomis's behaviour in Chapter 26.

Robert O'Brien's art in *Z for Zachariah*
The characters

Ann

I am hopeful

Ann Burden's character emerges fully and convincingly in her journal, so that by the end we have a clear picture of a many-sided and quite remarkable personality. It is one of the deepest ironies in the book that Mr Loomis is unable to appreciate his good fortune in meeting someone of her equable temperament and rare blend of accomplishments. She comes across to the reader as someone who is at once practical yet sensitive; self-contained yet companionable; vulnerable yet resilient; realistic yet spiritual; stoical yet hopeful; and generous yet cautious. It is out of these seemingly opposing characteristics that Robert O'Brien has fashioned a character who lives and speaks in her own right, quite independently of the writer who created her.

O'Brien dramatizes an extreme situation in which two people are freed from the restraints of civilized society and have to rely upon their own inner resources to help them shape and order their lives. Ann has been given a soundly balanced character by her upbringing, whereas Mr Loomis lacks these spiritual qualities. This contrast between the two characters leads us to consider the contribution the humanities and science make to the enrichment of human life.

Ann's imagination has been richly fed by the Bible and great works of literature. They have clearly had a profound influence upon her, developing her sense of beauty, providing moral precepts, emphasizing the importance of human relationships, enlarging her idea of the spiritual world beyond herself and offering consolation in times of doubt and depression. To put it another way, in the words of the Bible, 'man cannot live by bread alone'. In order to live satisfactorily, Ann needs to feed her mind just as surely as she needs to feed her body. She can survive without books, but she would feel diminished without them.

Through the character of Ann, then, Robert O'Brien shows the inner self-assurance which comes from practical self-sufficiency and the humanizing influence of the arts. It is important to note, however, that although Ann likes poetry, she is no idle dreamer. She is capable of planning ahead in a briskly efficient manner, but O'Brien seems to be hinting that while plans are essential to our lives, they should not occupy us totally. They are a means to an end, not the end itself.

Ann's background and upbringing occupy a central position in an understanding of her character. Born of generations of farming stock, she embodies many of the traditional values of farmers everywhere: self-reliance, respect for the land, acceptance of hard work and love of simple pleasures. In the modish world outside the farming community, these values are easily scorned. On one occasion, in Chapter 8, Ann herself reveals that the boys of Ogdentown considered country girls like her to be unfashionable. But when set against the extraordinary fate to which she is born, such attitudes are shown to be priceless.

One benefit is that they allow her to accept the inevitable without degenerating into self-pity. Farmers have to live with the constant likelihood of unforeseen disaster: too much rain can ruin a crop just as surely as too little; disease can infect even the most carefully tended stock. All farmers know that there is a point beyond which prudence and good husbandry are of little avail because they are at the mercy of natural forces which they cannot control. Ann knows it, too, and in this she is like another farmer, Hardy's Gabriel Oak in *Far From the Madding Crowd*. Oak loses everything he owns but with the same kind of stoicism that Ann shows looks for work as an ordinary farmhand, even finding 'a dignified calm' in his ordeal.

O'Brien leaves us in no doubt of the profound sense of loss Ann feels over the death of her family. It is there in the pure joy she experiences in Chapter 5 when she dreams that her family are back in the house; it is there, also, in Chapter 16 after Mr Loomis has grabbed her roughly by the hand, when in her fear she imagines that she is not alone, that her parents are coming back with David and Joseph. These are virtually the only two occasions in the book when the matter is referred to, yet the reader is left in no doubt how cruelly she feels their loss. It is in keeping with Ann's character that she does not draw attention to her suffering; grief is something which is privately felt not publicly paraded.

The self-control she displays is an essential aspect of her character. In the incident mentioned above, when she imagines that her parents are coming back, she says that she put the matter out of her head 'as I have learned to do'. These last words are important, for they show that Ann's self-control is achieved by a powerful act of will. It is a condition which she generates in herself and is evidence of her enormous strength of mind. She has, we remember, faced not only the loss of her parents, but the death of the planet. There has been no one to offer comfort or consolation. In fact, the reverse has been true. The only human voices she has heard between the war and the arrival of Mr Loomis have been those of the radio announcers, and the last of these was so frightened that Ann knew something terrible was happening. Then, for months after the war, she expected the deadness to creep into the valley from outside (Chapter 6). As with so much of what she says, this is understated so that its full impact is felt only when we ponder the awful meaning behind the simple words. For a period after the war, Ann expected to die, utterly alone and in a manner of which she was entirely ignorant. That she has come relatively unscathed both emotionally and mentally through this ordeal is largely due to the stoicism and resilience natural to many country people which finds particular and dramatic expression in Ann's character.

One artistic problem which Robert O'Brien faces in presenting such resolute self-control in Ann is that her character might seem less than human, as if she is an automaton whose self-control is achieved because of an incapacity to feel. This is triumphantly not the case with Ann and part of her success as a character comes from the delicate balance O'Brien achieves between the control of her feelings and the strength of those feelings. Two examples from different ends of the book help make this point. In Chapter 3, when the stranger calls out, Ann feels an almost overwhelming rush of emotion. She wants to run to him, weeping with joy and relief and touch his face. The yearning she has for human company is obvious here, but immediately her sense asserts itself and she remains hidden. Prudence overrides desire; reason controls emotion. The second example occurs right at the end of the book, and shows Ann giving way more freely to her feelings despite an attempt to restrain herself. For more than a month, she has been in hiding, living in intolerable conditions, knowing that unless she does something drastic Mr Loomis will inevitably capture her. When she confronts him finally, the emotional strain shows. Initially she manages to contain her fear and speaks with care and restraint. However, on this last occasion, just as she is about to leave her home, she is overwhelmed by emotion, and her last words to Mr Loomis are, as she admits, childish. The brief outburst reminds the reader that Ann is both vulnerable and very young.

If her upbringing has endowed her with the strength of character to cope with the horrors which face her, it has also provided her with a bedrock of unshakeable morality. Once again, she might strike the reader as unfashionable in this respect, but her attitudes are not uncommon among farmers, perhaps especially those in America, many of whom settled there because of the chance it offered to live a simple rural life in accordance with their religious or moral beliefs. Ann's family seem to have been churchgoers, for in Chapter 4 she refers to her family attending the church in Ogdentown, and her graduation the year before the war from Sunday School to the real service. Furthermore, she often mentions the Amish who lived in the next valley, and who were a Protestant sect whose ancestors left Europe to settle as simple farmers in America. In Chapter 11 Ann disclaims any suggestion that she is extremely religious, but she has obviously been raised in a locality where religious and moral beliefs have shaped and informed the values by which she lives. They permeate the novel in small and great events. When she first plays the piano for Mr Loomis in Chapter 7, we learn that she can play hymns better than anything else, and gains pleasure from doing so. More significantly, her thoughts on marriage to Mr Loomis in Chapter 8 take very conventional shape. One could argue that the notion of formal marriage has become obsolete in a post-holocaust world. However, she discounts even the merest possibility of simple co-habitation. They will be married in church in strict accordance with the ceremony as laid out in the *Book of Common Prayer*, even though there will be no minister present. Ann is adamant about that.

Perhaps the most dramatic manner in which her morality shows itself is in the high value she places on human life, in stark contrast to Mr Loomis's attitude. In the nightmare which follows his attempt to rape her, Ann has one distinct and fundamental advantage over him — she is a better shot than he is. In other words, she has the means of ending the progressively intolerable conditions under which she lives simply by shooting him. In such extreme circumstances it could scarcely be counted as murder. Yet it is a solution she never considers, no matter how extreme her own danger. Ann is no sentimentalist: she will readily kill animals for food but to kill to secure her own position is something she finds morally repugnant. Two examples will show how abhorrent she finds this kind of killing. The first occurs at the end of Chapter 23 when she considers herself to be a murderer simply by having intended to kill Faro, an intention which she could not put into practice. The second occurs in the final chapter. Mr Loomis stands with his back to Ann, who is hidden from sight. She has the perfect opportunity to rid herself of this menacing figure. But she knows that she cannot shoot him. Instead, she faces him, expecting him to shoot her. Implicit in her action is a belief that it is better to die than to live a murderer. As she faces his rifle, she feels not fear but disappointment, disappointment that after having worked so hard to keep things going she is now to die.

This reflects another aspect of Ann's character. Although she adapts well to a life of solitude, Ann's deepest satisfaction comes from being of use to others and experiencing joy in sharing. It is possible to see this as another manifestation of her traditional upbringing which has imbued her with a feeling of duty towards her fellow humans. The novel explores this character trait in two principal ways: specifically in her relationship with Mr Loomis; more generally in her thoughts on a career. We notice in Chapter 7, for example, that she feels proud to be of help to Mr Loomis when he rests his hand on her shoulder. It is a small but important glimpse of the self-fulfilment Ann finds in helping others. The excellent care she takes of him during his illness is a more sustained example, for she proves to be a caring and considerate nurse. Then, in Chapter 9, when she successfully starts the tractor, she hurries into the house to share the triumph with Mr Loomis. In Chapter 15, she feels like running into his room and applauding his attempts to walk. Even when there is little personal satisfaction to be gained, after their relationship has soured, her sense of duty prevails. In Chapter 21 she shares the chicken equally between them. In the next chapter, she scrupulously divides in half the three fish she has caught. Her behaviour here is all the more remarkable when we remember that Mr Loomis is systematically planning to deprive her of the means of living any kind of independent life.

The more general treatment is to be found in her wish to teach. Teaching offers Ann a means of simultaneously combining these two aspects of her character, for she will be able to share with her pupils her pleasure in books while at the same time she will be socially useful by helping to educate them. It is a desire which is so deeply embedded in Ann that it finds expression as a dream in Chapter 24 (page 74). Its emergence in the latter stages of the book is important, for it shows Ann's need for an objective in life for which to strive. The war put an end to her original wish for a career in teaching. The arrival of Mr Loomis gave her hope that together they could prolong the life of the planet (Chapter 9). Now that hope has died. It is replaced by a variation of her original thought. She dreams, repeatedly, of a classroom full of books and children wishing to be taught. The dreams might, of course, be a telepathic representation of reality. Perhaps there actually is such a valley. Ann certainly believes so. Equally likely, though, is that the dreams are the formulations of a deep, sub-conscious desire in Ann, given release in sleep when the conscious mind does not exert its usual control. Whatever their cause they provide Ann both literally and metaphorically with a sense of direction: literally for she dreams again the night after leaving her valley and awakes knowing which way to go; metaphorically for her life has new purpose and this new purpose gives her hope.

Ann's dreams (she has several in the book – see Chapters 5 and 8 as well) can also be seen as aspects of what might be called 'the life of the mind'. They are different from Mr Loomis's dreams, for whereas his are nightmarish re-enactments of what actually happened, Ann's are more imaginative and are usually expressions of what she most deeply wishes. It is this sense of an imagination needing to be fed (a 'life of the mind' as well as a life of the body) which characterizes Ann. As we have seen, she is adept at providing herself with food, but this practical day-to-day efficiency is wedded to a yearning for mental stimulation. Significantly, this takes its form through the highly personalized medium of literature, not the more impersonal form of science. Ann not only loves literature, she loves the best literature, and it is apparent that books for her are not simply a means of escapism (though they doubtless offer that as well) but a source of deep personal enrichment. We come to know the fine tuning of her mind through the books she likes. The sadness of Gray's *Elegy* might contrast with the bright, sparkling quality of *Pride and Prejudice*, but both works appeal to the discriminating mind by their poise and appeal to human dignity. They require a sympathetic and mature imagination to recreate in one's mind the events they describe and the 'worlds' they create. Evidence of Ann's ready imaginative sympathy is plentiful throughout the novel – her numerous references to 'poor Mr Loomis', for example, and the ease with which she identifies with Edward's dire predicament in Chapter 11. Such a mind as hers finds immense gratification in the pleasure of good books, and the refining of the imagination which occurs as a result enables her to understand more fully the sufferings both of Mr Loomis and Edward.

Her reading of the Bible, her prayers and her visits to church are further evidence of Ann's mental needs. What they have in common with literature is a sense of life outside and beyond oneself, a world one cannot see but which one creates in one's mind. Ann finds consolation and pleasure in such activity. As a consequence, she is less self-centred and frightened than Mr Loomis, seeing herself as part of larger whole, not an isolated fragment. It also helps us to understand how she can believe so firmly in the valley of which she dreams. She is used to entering the 'worlds' created by writers and according them a kind of reality. To accept the reality of her own dream is a small step.

Ann Burden is aptly named, for she carries burdens enough, yet her courage never falters. In the most unenviable of circumstances, her humanity remains intact; she becomes neither brutalized nor despairing despite the fact that the world outside her valley has participated in the ultimate folly. It is a world into which she travels with hope, sustained by her dream. In having her do so, Robert O'Brien suggests that no tragedy will ultimately quell the human spirit; that even in the most appalling circumstances imaginable, some of those who remain will see beyond their own needs to the needs of others, and will have the faith and the courage to seek to implement their dreams.

Mr Loomis

Don't leave me here alone.

Whereas we meet Ann Burden directly and come to know the minutiae of her thoughts and actions, we know Mr Loomis only from what she tells us of him. In other words, he exists at a further remove, and so our primary sympathy goes to Ann, and it is she with whom we identify. This is partly because we are sometimes uncertain how far we should sympathize with Mr Loomis, or even if we should sympathize with him at all. He is a murderer, after all, and his treatment of Ann can hardly be called considerate. The problem of how we approach his character is further compounded by his reticence about his background. We know what he does once he is in the valley because Ann tells us. Of his life before, we have only a little information, for he is notoriously unforthcoming, and what he reveals is mainly in the form of *facts* as opposed to his opinions and beliefs. This is to say that he tells us some of the outer, public events of his life, but little of his inner self. In order to build up a picture of him, of what this inner self is like, we have to piece together what he says and does and deduce from that what kind of person we think he is. Even then we cannot be absolutely sure, so sketchy is our evidence. Robert O'Brien clearly intends the reader to approach an understanding of Mr Loomis's character in this way; it is one reason for the choice of the first person narrative. The reader is forced to share Ann's ignorance and puzzlement without the provision of any satisfactory answers. There is no all-knowing third person author to step in and tell us what Mr Loomis is thinking, or why he is behaving as he is. We see him, as Ann sees him, from the outside. It is this refusal of Robert O'Brien to offer any neat, final solution to the character of Mr Loomis which aids the book's realism. Just as in real life we cannot predict the actions of other people or know what they are thinking, and just as we have to be careful not to misunderstand them when we examine their actions and look for a reason for them, so we are in the same position with Mr Loomis.

Before we begin to look more closely at the kind of man he is, let us note some of the *facts* we learn about him before he entered the valley. His family was poor. We do not know where he was born, but he used to visit a cousin who lived in a small town called Nyack in New York State. On these visits he used to enjoy listening to his mother's cousin play the piano. After leaving school he attended Cornell University, also in New York State, where he studied chemistry. For four years he worked for the navy in a laboratory in Bristol, New Jersey, specializing in the study of plastics. This led him back to Cornell where he became a postgraduate student working with Professor Kylmer, a Nobel prizewinner, on secret experiments to magnetize plastic. Perhaps the two most important details which emerge from this brief outline are: firstly the pleasure he felt in listening to the piano; and secondly his skill as a research chemist. Mr Loomis was evidently highly regarded in having a Nobel prizewinner invite him to join his team. The significance of these two points will emerge a little later, but for the present let us continue to create a picture of Mr Loomis from what we are told rather than from what we have to deduce. Let us move from fact to opinion, from what he tells Ann about himself to what she thinks of him, in the early stages at least. She thinks he is 'almost handsome' once he has cut his hair and beard; he has a long and narrow face with a rather large nose; he is quite tall; and he is, she thinks, aged about 30 or 32.

Having established these 'external' features of his character and background, let us begin to see what we can deduce about him. Let us look first at what we discover up to the time his illness is at its peak, and then see if what we have learned helps to explain his extraordinary behaviour thereafter.

Perhaps the first feature to be noticed on his entering the valley is his extreme caution. He double checks the radiation level, and approaches the farmhouse with noticeable circumspection. This caution is understandable, and is a characteristic – one of the few – which he shares with Ann. We notice, too, by the way in which he kills the chicken, that he is unused to living off the land, and from this we can deduce that his knowledge of farming and self-sufficiency are limited. An element of mystery is introduced in Chapter 5 with his mention of Edward and bullets, but the full effect of what this means is not made apparent yet. In Chapter 5 we learn too of the calm way in which he accepts the possibility of his dying from radiation poisoning. A possible explanation for this calmness appears in the next chapter. His work has given him a detailed knowledge of the effects of radiation poisoning. He knows exactly what he faces, and because he knows he can confront it; it is ignorance of what might happen which can cause uncontrollable fear. Chapter 6 also suggests a radical difference between Mr Loomis and Ann in their attitude towards science. Ann's view of scientists is that they will never accept things as they are; they always have to find an explanation for them. A little later she says that she does not find his discovery of a way of magnetizing plastic to be especially exciting, although she can see that a government would. Their dissimilar attitude to science is not merely a superficial difference between them. It is fundamental because it affects the way in which they think and see the world and each other: Mr Loomis as a scientist, and Ann as someone more sympathetic to the humanities.

Although it becomes most frightening in the second half of the novel, this difference is evident early on. There is, for example, Mr Loomis's suggestion that Ann use the petrol in Klein's store to run the tractor. His comment that she can operate the pumps manually as there is no electricity makes her feel stupid for it had not occurred to her. She is not stupid, of course. It is merely that Mr Loomis's scientific training has made him mechanically knowledgeable. Ann is practical, but not mechanical. His competence and interest in technology are further evident when he proposes building a generator and using the waterfall to provide the power. She finds books which interest him – *The Farm Mechanic* and a *World Almanac* which has diagrams of motors, pumps and wiring systems. Once again, we notice how this interest in mechanization contrasts with Ann's love of literature. For him books are purely a source of information; for Ann they help her understand and come to terms with life.

The contribution the arts and the sciences can make to the way we live is obviously an important theme in the novel. The arts give us a rich imaginative life, and develop our sympathetic identification with other people. O'Brien seems to be less sure about what the sciences offer. Obviously, technology can make Ann's life much simpler. Mr Loomis's advice on how to operate the petrol pumps, and his plans to generate power through a hydro-electric system are invaluable. But O'Brien does not let us forget that the world in *Z for Zachariah* has been annihilated through the misappliance of scientific knowledge. Even though Mr Loomis was working on a suit which would save lives, he too is part of this scientific community who are detached from the simple, enduring human values which O'Brien gives Ann.

One of the features of the scientific method is its impersonal quality. The emotions of the scientist have no bearing upon the work he does. This detachment seems to have spilled over into Mr Loomis's relationship with people and certainly with Ann. When she gleefully tells him that she has managed to start the tractor, for example, his manner surprises her; he is startlingly 'matter-of-fact'. We begin to wonder if the study of science has denied him an opportunity to develop the emotional side of his nature. It is there, of course, as Ann's piano playing in Chapter 7 makes clear. The evening is the best he has ever spent, he says. This obviously makes us wonder what kind of life he could have lived. We have no means of knowing, but the inference is that it has not been a life of rich personal fulfilment. We notice, too, his eagerness to go fishing and his embarrassment when he tells Ann that he has never been before. There is no reason why he should have, but his embarrassment is important because it suggests that he himself feels his life has been narrow in experience. It is even possible that as a man he feels a sense of personal inadequacy alongside the teenage girl whose skills in survival are greater than his.

While he can exercise a degree of emotional self-control in his waking hours, he has no control over his subconscious mind and it is in his dreams that the torment he suffers is most fully revealed. He is filled with guilt at what he did to Edward; his 'desperate groan' and 'strangling noises' after his dream in Chapter 12 show a mind in an acute state of trauma. Yet, when he is delirious, he is haunted by a fear that Edward will return to plague him, and attempts to shoot at someone who is already dead. The ferocity of these two emotions – guilt and fear – make any kind of personal equilibrium difficult to achieve and almost impossible to maintain. We must remember, too, that the ordeal he has been through since the war is even more horrifying than anything Ann has experienced. The insoluble position he found himself in with Edward – two men, one suit and a poisoned world outside – is only one aspect of this. He has actually travelled through that world and observed the devastation which Ann can only imagine. At the Air Force base, he had seen the desperate struggle between civilians and service personnel as they fought each other for a place in the safe-room. And having travelled for nine months and finally found somewhere safe he has, by a cruel irony, jeopardized his life by bathing in contaminated water.

The impact of all this upon Mr Loomis is something we can only estimate, never finally know. Yet it seems likely that a series of such extreme and inhuman experiences would harden aspects of his own nature rather than soften them, and drive him to extremes rather than to moderation. And this is exactly what happens. Mr Loomis's conduct in the latter part of the novel – from the time of his recovery – is a grotesque extension of what we know of him already; it is not a new development.

In the character of Mr Loomis we are shown a representative of modern society who is rootless, separated from the world of nature and with no spiritual principles to guide him. He is not an evil man, but a man whom fear can make behave in an inhuman way, in a way Ann never would. The circumstances of Mr Loomis's life have not provided him with the inner resources to cope with the horrors which face him. With his impoverished imagination, he has no dreams to inspire him and no ethics to guide him. Consequently, he flounders.

In the safe-room with Edward he chose to live at the expense of Edward's life. It was an act of selfishness (which must be contrasted with Ann's conduct in the final chapter), but perhaps understandable if not pardonable. Now he proposes to live at the expense of Ann. There is no need for this, as the valley can sustain both of them, and Ann would be an excellent companion. But the primitive instinct to survive overwhelms him and muddies his vision. Survival, his own survival, is paramount, and it is where the difference between himself and Ann becomes most extreme. She becomes rather like a piece of equipment which can be utilized to sustain his life. In other words, his attitude towards Ann becomes a perversion of the same detached approach he brings to science and technology; he regards her, and is willing to use her, in the same way that he would use the motor to drive the generator.

This begins to be apparent in Chapter 14 when he quizzes Ann on the planting of the garden. (His concern is a legitimate one; it is his tone which arouses suspicion). What is disturbing is his dismissive attitude towards her churchgoing during his illness, for we begin to glimpse that what Ann desires and needs is unimportant alongside what he needs. The gulf between them widens when, in Chapter 15, she mentions the shelves of Dickens, Shakespeare and Hardy in Ogdentown library. Mr Loomis's argument – that the suit is too important to risk on such a foolish expedition – can be seen as perfectly reasonable. However, it reveals his refusal to concede that books, and the enlargement of the imagination which they offer, are not peripheral to Ann's life; they are central to it. She can survive without them, but she is not fully alive. When, at the end of the chapter, Mr Loomis speaks of working for the future, Ann finds little pleasure in his words, and the reason is not far to seek. Her vision of working for the future was larger and more imaginative than his. She hoped to prolong the life of the planet, or part of it, and the thought filled her with joy. He hopes merely to plan the future in order to provide sufficient food; his vision does not extend beyond this limited purpose.

The poverty of imagination he displays here is apparent also in the callous way in which he denies Ann any kind of separate, dignified humanity. He seeks to relegate her both physically and emotionally to someone merely who satisfies his needs: physically in the way in which he seeks to enslave her, and actually attempts to violate her sexually; emotionally, with cruel yet deadly insight, when he forces her to do the two things which give her greatest pleasure – reading and playing the piano – in obedience to his will. His lack of compassion, which seems to be the consequence of a stunted imagination fuelled by scientific training, contrasts vividly with Ann's treatment of him. Even when she is living in the cave once more, she brings him food because she cannot let him starve.

Without the imaginative and spiritual resources of Ann, Mr Loomis's idea of what makes an adequate life, even in a post-holocaust world, is remarkably circumscribed. Unable to see beyond himself, he has nothing to sustain himself when his world collapses. He can face death from radiation poisoning with a degree of dignity because he knows what it involves. It is having to shape a new life and discover a new purpose which he finds frightening. Unlike Ann, he has no dreams to inspire him. His idea of life is the mundane provision of food for the body. Yet in the final chapter he comes to recognize that Ann needs rather more than that. He moves from being a ruthless egoist to being a bewildered, frightened man, terrified of loneliness. His final act, though, is an act of generosity as he points Ann in the direction in which he saw birds circling. We cannot know what makes him do it – perhaps it is in gratitude to her for nursing him through his illness, or perhaps it is simply an attempt to offer help to a fellow human being. Either way, it suggests that perhaps Mr Loomis has taken the first important step away from spiritually corroding selfishness towards a saner and more dignified view of himself as a human being.

Z for Zachariah and its genre

Like any good book, *Z for Zachariah* is difficult to assign to a specific category of novel. The book reviewer Naomi Lewis, writing in the *Observer*, referred to it as 'science fantasy' because it is set in a period after a cataclysmic nuclear war. It might be helpful, therefore, to consider it first of all as a work of science fantasy, or science fiction as it is more commonly known, while acknowledging that it is remote from the kind of book dealing with alien beings, distant galaxies and spectacular technology. In an introduction to a science fiction anthology entitled *The Stars and Under*, the writer Edmund Crispin said, 'A science fiction story is a "what would happen if . . .?" story. What would happen if people lived to be a thousand? If moon and earth collided? If a man could go back in a Time Machine and alter the course of history?' Or, we might add, if a stranger entered a valley which had been unaffected by a nuclear war?

Of course, any kind of story is a 'what would happen if . . .?' story, but Crispin's point is a helpful one because it suggests that one of the staple ingredients of science fiction is that it deals with extreme events. So also do ghost stories and stories about magic, but Crispin distinguishes between them and science fiction by saying that science fiction is different in the type of explanation it offers for what happens. 'All fantasies (and science fiction is no exception) deal with happenings that are more or less strange, remote and unheard-of. Science fiction, however, is unique in that the explanation it offers is always 'natural' rather than 'supernatural'. This, again, helps our understanding of *Z for Zachariah* for although Mr Loomis, as a scientist, does not know why the valley survived the holocaust, he believes that there is a rational explanation why it did. The emphasis upon the 'natural' in the book is what helps make it so compelling. It deals with a world which is at once remote yet familiar, and what has made it remote is a problem which confronts us all – the possibility of nuclear war.

Edmund Crispin also says, 'To some extent, science-fiction writers do in fact ask the reader to take the science as read.' That is, we are not meant to question how the time machine works in H. G. Wells's story of the same title. Neither are we in *Z for Zachariah* meant to waste time wondering how the valley survived the holocaust. In each case the Time Machine and valley provide a starting point for the writer: what is of real interest is not *how* it happened, but *what* occurs as a consequence. In this respect *Z for Zachariah* has much in common with a more modern novel, *Lord of the Flies* by William Golding. In his book, Golding casts away on a remote Pacific island a group of schoolboys who have been evacuated from England at the outbreak of a nuclear war. Although the plane carrying them to safety has crashed, they have survived because they were in a detachable passenger tube. Golding wastes little time on technical explanations and scientific probabilities. His real purpose is to show how a group of children will soon revert to primitive savagery once the restraints of civilizations have been removed. The fact that the civilized world has just engaged in a brutal war is only one of the many ironies which enrich the book. In the same way, the strength of *Z for Zachariah* does not lie in the way Robert O'Brien convinces us that the valley survived, but in the close study of the relationship between two strangers who believe they are the only people left on earth. Both O'Brien and Golding are, in their different ways, interested in human behaviour and motivation, especially when it is stripped of the protective clothing of civilization. For it is when there are no external, social restraints that one behaves as one truly is. The 'science' in the books of both writers is merely a means of getting rid of social restraints, of putting their characters *in extremis*.

If *Z for Zachariah* can be seen as belonging to a certain category of science fiction, it is also helpful to look at it as an 'island' novel. Among other such novels are: Defoe's *Robinson Crusoe*; Swift's *Gulliver's Travels*; Ballantyne's *The Coral Island*; Huxley's *Island*; and *Lord of the Flies*. Ann Burden might not be surrounded by water, but she is marooned just as surely as Crusoe is or Golding's schoolboys are. The idea of an individual or small group cast away is obviously an appealing one to a writer because the situation is immediately dramatic. Indeed the first three novels mentioned above might be seen as early examples of Edmund Crispin's 'What would happen if . . .?' kind of story, although in each case it is a shipwreck rather than the moon colliding with earth which gets the story underway.

'Island' novels can offer remarkable scope to writers: they can provide the opportunity for nothing more than a good adventure story as in *The Coral Island*; they can be used to satirize human folly as in *Gulliver's Travels*; they can present the author's vision of a perfect society as in *Island*; they can study the capacity for evil and barbarity at the heart of mankind as in *Lord of the Flies*; and they can show the inescapable solitariness of each one of us in relation to our fellow human beings and our need to accept this without degenerating into mere selfishness, as in *Robinson Crusoe*. This last point raises one or two areas of similarity between *Robinson Crusoe* and *Z for Zachariah* which are worth following. For instance, both writers adopt a plain first person style of narrative which makes fiction parade as fact. (*Robinson Crusoe* was actually believed to be an autobiography when it first appeared.) Both Ann and Crusoe are *in extremis*, he marooned on an island, she in her valley. Both are stoical about their plight. Although Ann feels keenly the loss of her family, she does not allow herself to be debilitated by it. Similarly, Crusoe says 'It was in vain to sit still and wish for what was not to be had, and this extremely rouz'd my application.' Both Ann and Crusoe are extremely practical about providing for themselves, yet neither of them sees this as the sole purpose in life. The spiritual side of Crusoe finds expression in religious faith, while Ann's conception of human purpose has been shaped partly by religion and partly by literature. The parallel does not hold good in all respects, of course; Crusoe finds contentment in the company provided by Man Friday, but Ann finds bitter disappointment in the company of Mr Loomis. And while Crusoe is rescued – after twenty-eight years two months and nineteen days – we are denied the comforting idea of Ann's salvation.

Each of the categories of novel we have looked at – science fiction and 'island' stories – provides some useful insights into the literary background of *Z for Zachariah*. However, the mark of a good book is not how easily it can be assigned to a genre, but how difficult it is to do so. Genres are large and impersonal; a good book will be the expression of a highly individualized interpretation of experience and will consequently elude any attempt to classify it once and for all.

Structure and style

Ann Burden's journal is so gripping in the story it tells that the reader is likely to forget that it is not a journal in the normal sense at all but a highly structured work of literature, written by a gifted novelist, which masquerades as the day-to-day, often hastily written account of a young person's harrowing experiences. The poet and critic Samuel Taylor Coleridge wrote that literature demands a 'willing suspension of disbelief' in an audience in order for it to succeed; that is, a reader must be prepared to enter imaginatively into the writer's world, to accept its conventions, and not judge its action simply against the 'real' world outside. This 'suspension of disbelief' is achieved so effortlessly in *Z for Zachariah* that it is easy to forget that we are reading fiction at all. Still, we must remember that its realism is purely illusory; it is a device employed by Robert O'Brien in order to increase its tension and to generate excitement.

Obviously, the choice of a journal as the means of telling the story is of enormous help here. We tend to think of a journal as a private, *factual* account of events, written only for the eyes of the writer. It is not written for public consumption in the way that a novel is. Ann herself explains in Chapter 1 that the reasons she is keeping her journal are firstly because she was forgetting when things had happened or even if they had happened at all, and secondly that writing a diary might be like having someone to talk to. The first reason is particularly interesting when we consider how writers try to give us an illusion of reality. We have all forgotten dates when things have happened to us, and it is easy enough to confuse what has happened with what we thought happened. It is therefore simple enough to understand Ann's reason for keeping a journal. But of course Ann Burden is a fictional character, and the journal technique, is a clever piece of technical expertise by Robert O'Brien. By casting the novel in journal form he immediately enhances its sense of realism, and helps make it that much easier for the reader to suspend disbelief and enter into a fictional world. We believe that we are reading autobiography rather than fiction.

Of course Robert O'Brien is not the first writer to do this. For example, in *Huckleberry Finn*, written in 1884, Mark Twain begins the book by having Huck say

You don't know about me without you read a book by the name of *The Adventures of Tom Sawyer*, but that ain't no matter. That book was made by Mr Mark Twain, and he told the truth, mainly. There was things which he stretched, but mainly he told the truth . . .

Huck then proceeds to tell of his adventures, which are the entire 'truth', without any 'stretching' because this time he, not 'Mr Mark Twain', is the one who is writing. But of course it is Mark Twain who guides the events and characters of his novel *Huckleberry Finn* just as surely as Robert O'Brien does with *Z for Zachariah*. Both writers are making fiction seem like fact.

O'Brien's choice of a journal as the literary form in which to tell the story has another advantage besides realism: the reader is always aware of the time-scale in which the events occur. In this respect, the structure of the book is purely chronological. It begins in the middle of May and ends in early August. Nothing could be more straightforward it seems. But even this apparently simple and realistic method conceals the careful, shaping hand of the novelist. Set against this fairly limited time-scale there is the subtle use of flashbacks which widen the chronology of the novel. In Chapter 1, for instance, Ann informs us of the circumstances leading up to her present life; in Chapter 5 she describes the family outings to church; in Chapter 6 Mr Loomis tells of his work as a chemist prior to the war. There are countless other examples where the forward movement of the story is halted and we are taken back in time. This has a twofold effect. Firstly it provides invaluable information on the character of Ann and Mr Loomis, and secondly it accentuates the comparative speed with which the events of the novel occur. It is as though there are two time-scales in the book: the longer one, in which Ann and Mr Loomis can refer to events which occurred earlier in their life, and the shorter, more intense one of their life together where circumstances can change alarmingly on a daily basis.

However, whereas a real journal might be a rambling, disorderly affair filled with random jottings, the tightness of the construction of *Z for Zachariah* is evident from the start. One of Robert O'Brien's favourite techniques is the use of the 'hook' in order to stimulate the reader's desire to read on. The first two sentences provide a ready example, but there are dozens of others in the book. Sometimes a startling or dramatic statement begins an entry and the events leading up to it are then fully explained. Look, for instance, at the first paragraph for May 25th and consider the questions it raises in our minds. What mistake has the stranger made? Has he made a mistake? If so, how bad is it? To find out we read on. The same kind of device is used at the beginning of Chapters 11, 16, 17, 18, 21, 23 and 25. It is noticeable that they occur more frequently as the novel enters its tense latter stages. But such 'hooks' are not confined to the beginnings of chapters or individual entries. Look, for example, at the mysterious first words the stranger utters in Chapter 5; his reaction at the end of Chapter 6 when Ann mentions Edward's name; the continuing mystery of Edward at the end of Chapter 10; her comment in Chapter 17 that everything was normal until dinner time; her statement in Chapter 21 that she was wrong to believe she had escaped suspicion when she returned to the cave; another statement a little later in the same chapter that she was wrong in thinking that Mr Loomis had removed the tractor key in order to conserve petrol. As a structural device such 'hooks' are simple enough, but there is no doubting their effectiveness in enticing the reader to read on.

Another feature of the structure of the book which must be noticed is the viewpoint from which the story is told. It is a first person narrative, inevitably so as it purports to be a journal. This naturally affects the way in which the reader approaches the book. Instead of having an omniscient narrator who can keep us abreast of all the events in the novel, we are given only a limited viewpoint – Ann Burden's viewpoint. For one thing, this ensures that we identify closely with Ann. We come to know her well: we share her fears, understand her doubts, admire her courage. The extent to which we imaginatively participate in Ann's life is a measure of the novel's success. A good example of the way in which the use of the limited viewpoint can work to advantage occurs in Chapters 17 and 18. In Chapter 17, by a subtle exercise of will, Mr Loomis makes Ann read to him and then falls asleep. In Chapter 18 she has to play the piano for him and there is the incident where he appears to drop his stick. His behaviour puzzles her. Why should he ask her to read when he does not want to listen? Why should he try to frighten her by making her believe he is creeping up on her as she plays the piano? Is he trying to frighten her? Perhaps his stick actually did fall to the floor and there is nothing sinister to it at all. Ann says that it 'did not look as if it had slipped.' The word 'look' is important here, for she cannot be sure. And neither can we. So her uncertainty, and ours, is intensified. Had the novel been written in the third person by an omniscient narrator we might feel at this point that we are being artificially denied information in order to generate suspense, rather in the way we are in an Agatha Christie thriller. There is no such 'cheating' here. Ann can only tell us what she knows and thinks. Its very inadequacy is both realistic and compelling.

The use of the first person narrative naturally influences the way we see Mr Loomis. This has already been examined when we studied his character, but it is worth noting again here that Mr Loomis does not exist for us outside Ann's perception of him. It is easy enough for her to describe what he looks like and what he does – at least when she can see him. But she can never be certain of what he is thinking. We, too, can never know what makes him behave in the way he does and are tantalized by our partial knowledge of him. We are as disappointed as Ann is when he is so unforthcoming about his past in Chapter 16. Yet our very frustration is an essential ingredient of the novel. There are no cosy answers, and there is no all-knowing author to satisfy our curiosity. By choosing a first person narrative method, Robert O'Brien has made one of the two characters in the story as much of a mystery to the reader as he is to the only other character in the book.

A careful reading of the book will reveal that it has a cyclical structure as well as a linear one. The linear structure is the fairly straightforward chronological one in which the novel begins at point A (when Ann first sees the smoke from the stranger's camp fire) and ends at point B (when she leaves the valley), allowing of course for some flashbacks. However, there is another way of looking at the structure, which reveals how carefully the book has been built. It is possible to divide it roughly into three sections. In the first, Ann is hiding in the cave observing the movements of the stranger as he enters the valley and, later, the farmhouse. The second section covers the time in which they both live in the house. It embraces the stranger's illness, Ann's attentive care of him, and his callousness towards her which culminates in the attempted rape. In the final section Ann is once more hiding in the cave, watching Mr Loomis. It is interesting to note how so many of the ideas and incidents presented in the opening section re-occur, often in bleak and uncanny form, in the second and third sections, but especially the third, when the relationship between Ann and Mr Loomis deteriorates most markedly.

Some examples will serve to illustrate the point. In Chapters 1 to 4 inclusive, Ann makes the following observations, among others:

1. what if a car came over Burden Hill and she ran out to greet it only to discover that the driver was mad, brutal or a murderer? (Chapter 1);

2. this makes her wary of the approaching stranger because she believes that there are worse things than loneliness (Chapter 1);

3. while still hidden from the stranger she feels it is the beginning of the end (Chapter 2);

4. she watches him using her house, building a fire with her wood and killing one of her chickens (Chapter 3);

5. Faro returns and, to Ann's horror, finds her tracks and races through the trees towards the cave (Chapter 4);

6. Ann worries that because the stranger is bigger and stronger than she is, he might make her his slave (also Chapter 4).

Each of these is echoed and developed in later sections of the novel.

1. Ann actually calls him *insane* (Chapter 24), although his behaviour before that has convinced the reader that he is severely emotionally and mentally disturbed; his *brutality* is apparent most graphically of all when he tries to rape her at the end of Chapter 18; and in Chapter 11 she learns that he is a *murderer*;

2. at the end of Chapter 20 Ann muses that her life now is so appalling that she wishes Mr Loomis had never come to the valley. She admits to having been lonely, but thinks that loneliness is preferable to what she is enduring;

3. her few months spent with Mr Loomis are so traumatic that they are the beginning of the end for Ann in the sense that she eventually leaves the valley in which she has spent her entire life;

4. from chapter 19 on she spends much of her time watching Mr Loomis's movements;

5. at the beginning of Chapter 20, she states that Mr Loomis intends to use Faro to track her, and in Chapter 23 he actually does;

6. in Chapter 16, when he has chairs placed on the back and front porch so that he can watch Ann working, she says he is like 'an overseer' – a word used in America especially of guards on slave plantations. The fear she expressed in Chapter 4 is now uncomfortably close. In Chapter 20 Ann imagines him tying her up in her house as he has already done to Faro. Later Mr Loomis tries to maim Ann so that he can enslave her.

It is as though the first part of the book presents the most nightmarish possibilities that could confront Ann, and the final part shows those possibilities becoming actualities.

Two other examples of this 'echoing' effect must be mentioned. The first concerns the similarity in the predicament between Ann and Edward. It begins to emerge clearly in Chapter 13 when Ann thinks of all the books in Ogdentown library and wonders if Mr Loomis would lend her the safe-suit to travel there. She stops short, for she remembers what happened to Edward when he wished to use the suit. In Chapter 14, when Ann is rash enough to mention the idea to Mr Loomis, she notices that some of the angry words he uses are identical to those he used, in his dream, to Edward. Ann's position seems to be a replication of Edward's, for she is trapped in the valley with Mr Loomis just as surely as Edward was trapped in the bunker. Finally, like Edward, she dons the suit and faces Mr Loomis's gun. There the parallel ends, but it has served to tighten the structure of the novel by dramatizing a predicament which, although different in appearance, is similar in essence.

The second example concerns the two evenings when Ann plays the piano for Mr Loomis (Chapters 7 and 18). Taken together, they provide a structural balance which allows the reader to gauge the shift in their relationship and the dashing of Ann's hopes of a happy future together. When Ann first plays for him he is ill and weak and utterly dependent on her. He announces that it has been the happiest evening he has ever spent. Ann excuses his angry comment a moment later, although the careful reader does not. In Chapter 18, the entire mood of the occasion is different. Ann is frightened and Mr Loomis has the initiative, in terms of mental strength at least. The culmination of this chapter is the attempted rape.

The style of Z for Zachariah is principally factual and plain as becomes what is supposed to be a journal written by a sixteen-year-old. Highly metaphorical language would be quite out of place in such a book. In fact, its plainness is one of its great strengths, for as well as enhancing its feeling of authenticity, it facilitates the stylistic device of understatement. On occasions throughout the book, Ann makes simple comments which strike the reader forcefully by the enormity of their implications rather than the power of the language. One or two examples will serve to make the point. In Chapter 1 she says that she hopes the stranger will not enter the valley and then everything will be all right again. By everything being 'all right' Ann means that she will continue to live a life of complete isolation imprisoned in a valley which she can never leave. The understated comment is at odds with the idea it conveys and very effectively makes the reader aware of what Ann now considers to be 'all right'. Another example occurs in Chapter 3 when she states almost in passing that all the songbirds are gone, by which she means they are dead. There is no crude attempt to shock the reader into realizing what it must be like to live in a world so unnaturally silent; the understatement allows the enormity of the idea to develop from within the reader's imagination rather than be bludgeoned from without by sensationalized, over-dramatic description.

One metaphorical sequence worth noticing, though, is the symbolic weight given to the crabapple tree. It is first mentioned in Chapter 8 (in a sequence which is among the most delicately evocative in the book) and its blossom is associated with Ann's hopes for marriage to Mr Loomis. When the tree is mentioned next, in Chapter 12, its blossoms have wilted, and so have Ann's hopes of the prospect of a happy, uncomplicated future – she knows that Mr Loomis is a murderer. Finally, in Chapter 21 when she is hiding from Mr Loomis, she passes the crabapple tree once more and notices the young green apples on its branches. The symbolic suggestion here seems twofold: firstly that the natural cycle has proceeded quite indifferent to the tense struggle between Ann and Mr Loomis; secondly that Ann's relationship has borne bitter fruit — where she once hoped for marriage she now fears enslavement.

A final point about the style concerns the description of the chase in Chapter 23 and the ransacking of the cave. We notice that as Ann begins to re-live the nightmare she moves from the past tense into the present. She has used the present tense occasionally elsewhere, usually at the start of chapters, but it is sustained here over several pages. Its purpose is clear. By re-living the events of the nightmare, Ann actually creates its horror for us. She does not merely describe what happens, she re-enacts it so that we seem to experience the action directly as it happens. It is a stylistic device which makes for compulsive reading.

General questions

1 Write brief biographies of Ann and Mr Loomis until the time that he enters the valley, using material from different parts of the book, and then discuss the ways in which their background differs.

2 Write a short play about the events leading up to Edward's death. Base your account on what happens in Chapter 11. You may use the dialogue in the book, but include your own, too, basing it on the description of events that Ann gives.

3 Why is the safe-suit so important? You might wish to consider the following points while thinking of your answer:

Mr Loomis's safe arrival in the valley;

his dreams and the patched bullet holes;

his behaviour when Ann asks to borrow the suit;

his reaction when he discovers that she has taken it.

4 Choose two incidents in the novel which you find particularly effective in presenting tension and show how Robert O'Brien achieves this tension.

5 Imagine that you are Mr Loomis. Using material from the book describe your entry into the valley from the time when you tear the leaves from the branch in Chapter 3 to the end of Chapter 4.

6 Read Ann's entry for May 27th and then answer these questions.

(a) What do we learn of Ann from her attitude toward Faro?

(b) Show how and why Ann's attitude toward Mr Loomis has changed.

(c) Choose one other occasion when a dream is important and show why it is so.

7 Select two incidents from the book, one which shows Ann's practical nature and one which shows her love of literature. Use them as the basis to write about these two aspects of her character.

8 In what ways are the two evenings when Ann plays the piano for Mr Loomis similar and different?

9 What part does Faro play in *Z for Zachariah*? You might wish to consider some of these points in your answer:

the link he provides with the past;

his affection for Mr Loomis;

his affection for Ann;

the use to which Mr Loomis puts him.

10 Write about Robert O'Brien's portrayal of Mr Loomis from the time he recovers from his illness until he tries to rape Ann. You might wish to consider:

his obsession with having enough food;

his mental cruelty to Ann;

his attitude towards her need for books:

his attempt to dominate her physically.

11 What do you think Robert O'Brien gains by having Ann tell her own story?

12 Read Ann's entry for June 6th and then answer this question. What do we learn of Ann

(a) from her reasons for going to church;

(b) from her treatment of Mr Loomis?

13 Read Chapter 23 carefully and then write about how Robert O'Brien makes the reader want to read on. You might wish to consider some of these points:

the effect of the opening sentence;

Ann's attitude as she walks towards the farmhouse;

Mr Loomis's shooting at her and his reasons for doing so;

the description of the chase;

the effect of the final sentence.

14 Using material from throughout the book give, as far as you can, a *factual* description of Burden Valley, including the farm and its outbuildings.

15 Write about your attitude towards Ann Burden.

16 Read Chapter 21 from the time when Mr Loomis and Ann begin speaking to the end of the chapter. Then answer these questions.

(a) how does Mr Loomis make a calculated attempt to discomfort Ann?

(b) what evidence is there that he has been watching her closely?

(c) what do we, and Ann, learn of Mr Loomis's plans from this extract?

17 Taking the novel as a whole, how do you respond to Mr Loomis? You might wish to consider some of these points in your answer:

his guilty conscience at killing Edward;

the effect his journey through the deadness has had on him;

his liking of music;

his treatment of Ann;

his behaviour in the final chapter.

18 In what ways is the book more than merely an adventure story?

19 Ann claims that she is not particularly religious. What part would you say religion plays in the novel?

20 Dreams play an important part in the book. What do Mr Loomis's nightmares and Ann's dreams tell us about them as people?

Suggested guideline notes for question 20

Mr Loomis's nightmares vivid re-creations of something which happened, rather than fantastic, horrifying imaginings. Extent to which they recur tell us how deeply affected he is by what he has done, as does his reaction in final chapter when Ann tells him she knows. This suggests that under normal conditions he is not a violent man. However, nightmares also reveal that under stress becomes dominating and selfish, foul-mouthed and callous; prizes the safe-suit, and his own life, above Edward's life. Contrast Ann.

Ann's dreams not necessarily based directly upon past experience, but are expressions of her deepest longings. Part of her 'life of the mind'. In Chapter 5, for example, she dreams her parents are alive and feels immense joy. Shows indirectly how deeply she mourns their loss. Also shows how dreams affect the conduct of her life. Realizes through this first dream that the thought of a life of loneliness almost too much to bear, and so decides to help stranger. Series of dreams she has at end of novel have same effect. Reflect two deep-rooted desires: safe place to live and a sense of purpose to life. Impossible to know if her dreams are fantasies or 'visions'; i.e. expressions of sub-conscious need and nothing more, or mystical experiences which are actually true. No way of knowing – for her or for us. Important though that she trusts her dreams. Ann needs something to believe in; it is her dreams which sustain her. Contrast Loomis.

21 Imagine that you are Ann's father. Using the information he gives in Chapter 1, together with any other details that seem probable, write an account of what you saw outside the valley.

22 Write an account of any dream or dreams you have had which have seemed so vivid as to be true.

23 Compare the description of the hunt in Chapter 23 with any other hunt for a human being you have read about in a book. You might, for example, wish to look at the way Ralph is hunted in Chapter 12 of *Lord of the Flies*.

24 Describe an occasion when you felt frightened and utterly alone.

25 Compare Mr Loomis's attitude towards Ann in the second half of the book with another male character in a book you have read who treats a female character *either* just as cruelly *or* with love and consideration.

Further reading

Novels by Robert O'Brien

Report from Group 17 (Gollancz, 1971)
Mrs Frisby and the Rats of NIHM (Gollancz, 1972)
The Silver Crown (Gollancz, 1973)

Other books of interest

Racso and the Rats of NIHM by Jane Lesley Conly (Gollancz, 1986)
The Stars and Under ed Edmund Crispin (Faber, 1968)